IT   / DAY

D1649419

This book is due for return on or before the last date shown below.

7/01/02

17 OCT 2005

19. 9.05

WITHDRAWN

A *Letts* EXPLORE **Literature Guide**

First published 1997

Letts Educational
Aldine House
Aldine Place
London W12 8AW
0181 740 2266

Text © Sandra Langdon 1997

Typeset by Jordan Publishing Design

Text design Jonathan Barnard

Cover and text illustrations Ivan Allen

Design © BPP (Letts Educational) Ltd

Acknowledgements

Extracts (approximately 1500 words in total) from *Talking in Whispers* by James Watson (Victor Gollancz Ltd, 1983) © James Watson 1983 are reproduced by kind permission of Penguin Books Ltd.

Examination questions reproduced by kind permission of the Northern Examination and Assessment Board.

The answers supplied to the Exam Board questions are solely the responsibility of the author, and are not supplied or approved by the Exam Boards.

British Library Cataloguing in Publication Data
A CIP record for this book is available from the British Library

ISBN 1 85758 627 1

Printed and bound in Great Britain
Ashford Colour Press, Gosport, Hampshire

Letts Educational is the trading name of BPP (Letts Educational) Ltd

Contents

■ Plot synopsis

The day before the general elections in Chile, the car carrying popular folk singer Juan Larreta and his band to San Jose is forced off the road by Security. His charango player, Horacio, is killed instantly. Juan is beaten and arrested, but his son, Andres, escapes. Andres thumbs a lift to San Jose with twin puppeteers, Isa and Beto. Andres and Isa are immediately attracted to one another. They come to a road block and learn that the democratic candidate, Miguel Alberti, has been shot whilst making his last public speech. The Communists are blamed. The Junta declares a State of Emergency and a curfew is imposed. Isa invites Andres to stay with her and Beto in Santiago. On the outskirts of the city they narrowly escape being shot by the army.

Overnight the National Stadium in Santiago is transformed into an interrogation centre as truckloads of prisoners arrive. Andres goes there the next day and spots his father's guitarist, Braulio among the prisoners. An American photographer, spotted by the guards taking pictures, passes his camera to Andres.

Horacio's cousin, Diego, develops the film. The American's photographs reveal Alberti being shot by Security. Diego devises a plan to recover his printing press, which has been dissembled and hidden around the city.

Three days later Andres and the twins carry out the plan at the train station. Andres hides the parts of the press in a quarry on the outskirts of town, and shortly thereafter witnesses the shooting of several prisoners. Checking the dead for his father, Andres discovers the body of the American photographer, Don Chailey.

That night Andres takes refuge in a seminary. Government soldiers arrive in the middle of the night looking for a Resistance soldier, and Andres is arrested as he attempts to escape. Andres is tortured.

Isa visits the seminary. A nun gives her Andres' package containing the documents found on Don Chailey's corpse. Isa contacts an American reporter, Jack Normanton, who has arrived to investigate the disappearance of Don Chailey. They meet in a leisure park and she gives him copies of the photographs.

Half dead, Andres is released only after the torturer is informed that the priest from the seminary has died as a result of being tortured. Andres' broken body is dumped along the river. He is discovered the next morning by a farmer's daughter who takes pity on him. The farmer and his daughter take

Andres to the San Miguel market. Andres is convinced that he is dying until he hears that a puppet show is being performed. With the help of the farmer's daughter he conceals himself in the back of the twin's van. The twins finish their show and leave the market. Beto discovers Andres when they stop for lunch.

There are no signs of the thousands of prisoners recently detained, beaten and shot at the stadium when the Two Hemispheres Trophy competition is played. During the game, General Zuckerman, leader of the Junta, is shown an American newspaper carrying Don Chailey's photographs. At half-time Andres watches as Isa and Beto distribute leaflets also carrying the photograph and story of the Junta's assassination of Alberti. The people of Chile have started to resist. Andres does not know what has happened to his father, but he is hopeful.

SOUTH
AMERICA

SANTIAGO

C H I L E

The road from
Santiago to
San José

The House of Laughter

The Seminary of Our Lady of Mercy

San Cristobal

SANTIAGO

CERRO SAN CRISTÓBAL

CARRETERA PANAMERICANA NORTE

VIA NORTE SUR

PARQUE QUINTA NORMAL

AV GRAL O'HIGGINS (ALAMEDA)

Santiago stadium

Quinta Normal Park

Who's who in *Talking in Whispers*

Andres

Andres Larreta

Andres is presented as a heroic character in many ways. Firstly, he is brave. Although he enlists the help of the twins and Diego Rosales, it is really Andres who, amidst terrible danger, is responsible for the printing of Don Chailey's photographs and testimony of the Silver Lion's assassination. Secondly, he has integrity. He suffers terribly for what he believes in, but the torturers are unable to break his spirit and he survives his severe injuries. Thirdly, he is strong but sensitive. He has endured tragedy early in his life as his mother was murdered and his father imprisoned, but he never feels sorry for himself, thinking instead of music and poetry when he needs emotional inspiration. Fourthly, he is dangerous. He is a known enemy to the Junta, so he risks his life every time he is seen in public. He is also romantic. He falls in love with Isa. Finally, he is indestructible. He is described by many different characters as 'a cat with nine lives.'

Andres is the most fully realised character in the novel. Part of the story is told from his point of view, so that we are able to experience first hand what he is thinking and feeling during key scenes in the novel. Most importantly, his character matures during the story. In Chapter 1 he is concerned with honour, bravery and pride. When we first meet him, he wonders if he is a coward for hiding from the Junta whilst his father is beaten and arrested. Later he shows off how brave he is in front of Isa when he volunteers to look around the corner of the house to see where the army is. A little later, in Chapter 4, he is visibly nervous during the execution of Diego's plan at the train station. His character starts to grow up in Chapter 5 when he forces himself to search the bodies of the dead prisoners at the quarry. By the end of the novel he is wiser, but sadder.

Andres is also a more realised character in the sense that we are told more information about his background, family and appearance than any other character. Keep track of all of these details.

As readers, we respond most sympathetically to Andres, not only because of his terrible ordeal but because he is very human. He has shortcomings as well as many admirable personality qualities. Find examples in the novel when Andres is courageous, bad tempered, romantic, sensitive, out spoken, rude, dutiful, competitive, humorous, cynical, silly, clever and resourceful. Add as many other personality qualities with examples from the novel as you can.

Isa

Isa

Isa, short for Isabel, represents love. She is beautiful and Andres falls for her immediately. After losing everyone else, Andres still maintains the will to live through the power of Isa's love. Isa is also able to quell any rivalry between Beto and Andres through her love for each. She is strong, independent, intelligent, cool, clever, plucky, loving and sensible. She has moments of folly, such as when she wants to look for Andres before curfew is over, but they never last for long as she is very sensible and quick to see reason. She is a natural born leader and inspires trust and confidence. She has strong values and knows what is important to her. How do we know that friendship is important to her? What other qualities and values are important to her?

Beto

Beto

Beto is very different from Isa and sometimes it is hard to believe that they are not only related, but twins! He is the clown of the group. He does not take life too seriously and is usually easy going. Find examples in the novel where Beto is curious, generous, impetuous, emotional, angry, nervous, scared and jealous. What physical attributes do the twins share? Think about Beto's importance to the story.

It is interesting to note that the three central characters in the story are performers. As puppeteers, the twins are able to say things through their puppets, such as General Zuckero, that they would not be able to otherwise say. What other opportunities are the twins afforded by their profession?

General Zuckerman

General Zuckerman is based on General Augusto Pinochet, the leader of the army who overthrew the Allende government and then ruled Chile as a ruthless military dictator. A dictator is a ruler who has complete power. The Junta, including the CNI and the torturers, take their orders from General Zuckerman. What impression do you get of him from his appearance and the way he treats others?

Diego Rosales

Diego's character serves a two-fold purpose in this novel. Firstly, he represents the spirit of the old Resistance movement. Despite his horrific physical injuries as a result of torture, his determination to resist the Junta cannot be threatened or broken. Secondly, he is instrumental to the Resistance plot. It is his printing press which allows the youngsters to print Don Chailey's photographs and testimony. It is also Diego who thinks up the plan to recover the printing press.

The Snake and the Hog

The Snake and the Hog represent one extreme of the extent of the Junta's brutality. They are members of the Junta's elite secret police, the CNI, who are involved in the torturing of prisoners for information about the Resistance movement opposed to their regime. The Hog represents the blind physical brutality of the torturers as he is the one who carries out most of the physical beating on Andres. The Snake represents the emotional or mental brutality of the torturers as he gives the orders and asks most of the questions. Torture is both mental and physical. What kind of person would become a torturer? We are surprised by the Snake's reaction to Father Mariano's death for which he is accountable. He seems to be able to draw a moral distinction between breaking people down mentally and physically, and killing them. His reaction illustrates the double standards that people can hold. These double standards are behind much of man's capacity for inhumanity.

Miguel Alberti, 'The Silver Lion'

Miguel Alberti represents democracy. He is a gentle philosopher poet who scorns the Death Squads and vows to send the soldiers back to their barracks. He is based on President Salvador Allende who restructured Chile along socialist lines from 1970 to 1973, but was forced out of power in a *coup d'état* by the army. Alberti is the choice of the poor, but is a threat to the wealthy and the army as much of their wealth relies on foreign interests. Alberti, like Allende, would have decreased foreign ownership of Chile's natural resources and prioritised improving the living and working conditions of the poor. He is assassinated because he poses a threat to the army who are backed financially by the Americans. After his death, his presence is symbolised by his green panama hat which Isa wears. The fact that he is a poet and 'roused the people with his golden oratory', associates him with the other poets and singers who represent freedom from political oppression.

Juan Larreta

Juan is proof that 'the pen is mightier than the sword'. In his vocation as a folk singer, he poses a bigger threat to the Junta than armed Resistance soldiers. He influences people through his music, which mostly consists of songs of political and social protest. Even after protest singers such as Juan die, they continue to influence listeners through their recordings. Juan's music would appeal mostly to the poor as he fights their cause through his songs. The targets of his songs are the rich and powerful who reach their positions at the expense of the poor.

In the novel, we only see Juan at the very beginning when he is forced off the road, beaten and arrested by Security. We never get a sense of his appearance, but his presence is strongly felt throughout the rest of the novel, mostly through his songs and Andres' thoughts. Andres gets involved in the Resistance movement as a result of his father's disappearance. Just the mention of his name provokes a strong reaction, both positive and negative. He is equally loved by the poor and hated by the rich. What impression do you get of Juan's personality?

Juan's character strongly demonstrates the repressive powers of the Junta – they ban his music, burn his books and manuscripts, publicly denounce his good name and print lies about him in the newspaper.

Don Chailey

Don Chailey represents hope for the Resistance movement in two ways. Firstly, his photographs and eye-witness testimony are evidence that the Junta assassinated Miguel Alberti. Secondly, as an American citizen, his death will raise awareness in the United States of what is really going on in Chile, and how the Americans themselves are involved. This will cause human rights groups in America to put pressure on the American government and multi-national corporations to stop involvement in exploitation and oppression in foreign countries.

Father Mariano

Father Mariano represents the Catholic Church in this novel. The Catholic Church is a considerable force in Chile – between 85% and 90% of the population is Catholic. Many priests in Chile are what Andres refers to on page 80 as 'worker-priests'. These priests are dedicated to, and live alongside, the poor members of their congregations. There are, however, other priests who forsake the poor to serve the wealthy. It is this second type of priest which Juan attacks in a song on page 79. Father Mariano lives at the seminary, where priests are trained, so that he is neither type of priest. He is, however, sympathetic to the poor as he knows the twins, grew up with Horacio, allows Andres to stay the night and takes in the wounded Resistance soldier despite the orders of the Archbishop.

Father Mariano's death at the hands of the torturer serves two purposes in the novel. Firstly, it shows that the Church is not immune from the brutality of the Junta. Secondly, it is partially due to the news of Mariano's death that Andres is released by the torturers.

Jack Normanton

Jack Normanton serves as a character foil to Don Chailey, not in terms of personality, but in terms of fate. Like Chailey he is a journalist, but unlike Chailey, he returns safely to America. He is important to the Resistance plot as his character introduces an element of hope in printing the truth about the Silver Lion and Don Chailey's deaths in the paper. Like Chailey, he also represents the interests of foreign countries in exposing the human rights atrocities around the world. Finally, his conversation with Colonel Rugeros of the Ministry of Information in Santiago, further highlights the dishonesty and repressive power of the Junta.

Horacio Rivera

The senseless murder of Horacio prepares us for the assassination of the Silver Lion and the Junta's brutality against Chile's poor and innocent. Horacio is a poor but talented guitarist and charango player. He helped Father Mariano get the roof repaired by doing one-man shows to raise money for the seminary. What possible threat could such a kind man have posed to the Junta? Of course when he was shot, it was Juan who the Security were really after. Horacio's death represents how little military dictatorships value the lives of poor citizens, and the lengths to which they will go to get rid of possible threats to their regimes.

Braulio Altuna

Like Horacio's murder, Braulio's senseless beating is another example of the Junta's considerable brutality. Braulio's character, however, is important in the novel primarily as a plot device. It was Andres' recognition and witnessing of Braulio's beating at the stadium which resulted in his chance meeting with Don Chailey.

■ Themes and images in *Talking in Whispers*

Brutality

Brutality

Brutality refers to cruel and vicious behaviour. The agent of the brutality in this novel is the military Junta. The Junta performs a range of brutal actions. At the lower end of the spectrum they beat the prisoners. On the extreme end of the spectrum they torture and kill. In addition to these forms of physical brutality, they also inflict mental brutality. The lies that they print in the paper about Juan are a form of mental or emotional brutality. The fact that many people have no way of finding out what has happened to their loved ones who have disappeared is also a form of emotional brutality. The torturers indulge in physical brutality to break the bones and mental brutality to break the spirit of their victims.

Brutality is used by governments which rule by force, especially military force. Often these governments have leaders called dictators. Brutality is used as a form of oppression against rebellion. It is easy to control people, and to make them behave as the government desires, when the people are frightened about the consequences if they do not obey rules. It is hard to fight back when you have broken bones or when you are in fear of losing or hurting a loved one because of your actions. The Junta's leadership creates a reign of terror because it rules by force, especially brute force. Why is brutality essentially cowardly behaviour?

One branch within the Junta is the CNI, or secret police. These are the specially trained officers who carry out the torture. Some critics feel that the torture scenes go too far, but Watson feels that it is important that these scenes are included. Children are often the victims of these brutal military regimes. Watson hopes that young people reading this novel will become more aware of the political atrocities suffered around the world, especially by people of their own age, and he hopes that they will feel sympathy for, and solidarity with, their less fortunate counterparts. As we see in the novel, it is often the help and support of foreigners that provide hope for the victims of political brutality. How is the terrifying impact of the acts of brutality achieved? Which political ideology do you think Watson supports, rule by force or democracy?

Repression

Repression in political terms refers to limiting and controlling the rights and freedoms of individuals in society. Why would governments want to limit and control the rights and freedoms of their citizens?

Repression

In this novel the Junta uses several methods of repression. It takes over all forms of media, such as broadcasting and newspapers. Controlling the media serves a two-fold purpose. Firstly, it denies citizens the freedom of speech. Secondly, the Junta can control the information given to their citizens and even deliver propaganda. This allows the Junta to control what people know and think. To this end they also burn books and ban the publication and performance of Juan's songs.

The Junta bans all public assemblies and suspends the activities of political parties and trade unions. What threat would trade unions be to the Junta? The effect of banning public meetings of any form is to prevent people from getting together and discussing ideas. It is hard to organise a revolt, or even a resistance movement if you cannot even get people together. Even schools and workplaces are closed.

The Junta imposes a curfew all over the Republic. The curfew ensures that people cannot meet secretly during the night. It also provides a good excuse to arrest people. The Junta also sets up road blocks and spot checks. The brutally suffered by individuals who oppose the Junta is also a form of repression – repression through fear. People are afraid to resist because they fear the consequences.

The Junta also represses the information that is broadcast internationally. It makes it very difficult for foreigners to find out any information about missing foreign nationals. Don Chailey is beaten and arrested when he is caught taking photographs. Naturally, foreign journalists would fly to Chile to cover the elections and the assassination of the Silver Lion. The information they receive is controlled by the state in the form of press conferences which offer the party line only. If foreign journalists become a nuisance they are simply expelled from Chile. In many countries foreign journalists are intimidated, arrested, beaten and even killed. Why must military regimes repress foreign journalists?

The title of the novel, '*Talking in Whispers*', refers to the experience of living in a repressed society. Why is this an apt title for this novel? Look at the way this idea is developed throughout the novel.

Freedom/resistance

Freedom/ resistance

Through the Junta's schemes of brutality and repression, the Chilean people lose their democratic freedoms. These include human rights. The only hope they have for regaining their freedom is to resist the Junta's control. Successful resistance will lead to fighting back. In this novel there are few instances of collective resistance or fighting back, but we feel, towards the end of the story, that they are certainly on the increase.

The resistance movement begins with individuals such as Isa who become resentful of having to talk in whispers, but the crowd also plays an important part because there is power in numbers. It is the crowd at the San Miguel market which creates the opportunity for the twins to escape the Security. Explore other examples of the power of crowd's resistance, both physical and psychological.

An important form of resistance comes from the aid of foreign countries. If the people can get the truth of the situation, with evidence of the widespread social injustice, out to foreign democracies then they are likely to raise interest in the current political situation in Chile. These foreign democracies can put pressure on the Chilean government, through trade and international politics, to change its policies.

In *Talking in Whispers* it is especially important that the average American knows the truth about the Chilean government. Zuckerman's regime is backed by American investment to protect American business interests in Chile's natural resources. We see, however, that socially conscious Americans such as Don Chailey are treated no differently than the Chileans who resist. Don Chailey was trying to expose the brutality of the Junta to the American public. He wrote, 'The Americans must stop giving aid and succour to bloody tyrannies such as Zuckerman's. Our own fears are our worst enemies, not the reds ...' What reaction was Chailey hoping to achievement from his countrymen? Why would Don Chailey's murder have a greater effect on the average American than the murder of hundreds of Chileans?

The most striking feature of this novel is not the horror of the torture chamber, but the courage of the people who resist.

Triumph of the human spirit

Triumph of the human spirit

In this novel, as in life, people survive terrible suffering because they are able to lift their spirits above the physical situation. Usually this implies looking beyond one's own individual situation and acting on behalf of the good of a group. In this story, comradeship, loyalty and trust are central to the success of the Resistance movement. Isa and Beto feel comradeship towards Andres because their own parents have disappeared and they can sympathise with Andres' terrible feeling of not knowing what has happened to Juan. Father Mariano and Andres stay loyal to the Resistance movement by not giving away the real identity of the wounded soldier treated at the seminary. Andres, Isa and Beto begin to feel solidarity when they all laugh nervously about Orlando the Ostrich pecking people's noses in Chapter 1. List all of the other examples of comradeship, loyalty and trust in the novel. Why are these concepts so important to spiritual survival? Which other characters offer these qualities?

Andres also feels comradeship in the poems and songs he thinks of when he needs inspiration. These songs and poems express what he is feeling and help him not to feel alone in his suffering, and not to feel defeated or sorry for himself. All forms of art can lift our spirits beyond our material concerns and isolation and inspire our hearts.

The human spirit is a powerful force. Andres is able to survive his horrific torture by thinking of Juan and Isa.

What do each of characters represent for Andres? Adverse situations can bring out the best and the worst in human nature. Think of all the instances in the novel when individuals or groups help Andres.

Narrative style and technique

Narrative style, structure and technique

Much of the success of a novel is owed to the style it is written in as much as to its content. Narrative style refers to the type of novel it is, the choice of language and point(s) of view used to tell the story. Narrative structure refers to the structuring of events. This includes narrative devices such as foreshadowing, flash backs and juxtaposition. Narrative technique refers to the author's skill in presenting the story and achieving the desired effects. All of these things play an important part in the telling of the story of *Talking in Whispers*.

Background to *Talking in Whispers*

The indigenous people to Chile are the Araucanian Indians. In the fifteenth century the Inca Indians moved into northern Chile. The Spanish conquered Chile in the sixteenth century and ruled it as a colony for three hundred years. Chile finally won its independence in 1818, led by Bernardo O'Higgins.

Chile is rich in nitrate, copper and iodine. First the British and, more recently, the Americans have been interested in Chile's natural resources. From the 1950s to the 1970s American multi-national corporations dominated Chile's industries. The people of Chile felt that these companies were reaping the benefits of the natural resources, while they suffered with low wages and poor working conditions.

In 1970, the Popular Unity Party, led by Salvador Allende, was elected to power. Allende's government brought about many reforms which improved the standard of living for Chileans.

The multi-national companies were threatened and feared other South American countries in which they had interests might follow Chile's example. The United States protected their interests by destabilising the Chilean government through economic boycotts, anti-Socialist propaganda and infiltration, and finally military force.

On the 11th of September 1973 the army, backed by American money, overthrew Allende's Marxist coalition government. Allende died in combat in the presidential palace. The Junta took power under the dictatorship of Augusto Pinochet. A constitution returning Chile to democracy took place in 1981. Pinochet was president of Chile until 1990. Patricio Aylwin was president from 1990 to 1994. The current leader, Eduardo Frei Ruiz-Tagle started his six-year term of office in 1994.

Talking in Whispers is set sometime between 1973 and the future, but it is based on the events of 1973.

The importance of songs and poetry

When Andres needs inspiration, he recalls many songs and poems of protest by Chilean artists. He thinks of songs by his father Juan and Chico Buarque, and a poem by the famous Chilean poet, Pablo Neruda. The title of the book is taken from a song by Chico Buarque. Juan Larreta is based on the famous Chilean folk singer, Victor Jara. Jara was arrested, tortured and murdered by the Junta in 1973. How do these songs and poems make Andres feel? Beto also recalls one of Juan's songs to celebrate the success of Diego's plan at the train station. Usually Juan's songs are inspirational. Father Mariano points out to Andres that one of his recent popular songs makes fun of the Church. The song began:
When the church men dine
At the richman's table
The poorman's sure
To go without.
Who is Juan's target in this song? Francisco, the farmer, also sings one of Juan's songs. When Andres hears the song, he sees it as a foothold when he thinks he is dying in the back of the farmer's van. What do the songs and poems represent for the people who remember them?

Human rights

The United Nations agreed The Universal Declaration of Human Rights in 1948. This consists of thirty articles of fundamental rights beyond those prescribed in law, that all individuals possess by virtue of their humanity. These include Article 5: Right to freedom from Torture; Article 9: Right to Freedom; Article 19: Right to freedom of Opinion; and Article 21: Right to Political Activity. It is not a legal document, but members of the United Nations, such as Chile, have the responsibility to honour it. Throughout the book many human rights are violated, such as those listed above. Note, too, that Andres had been expelled from his school for being involved in subversive activities as chairman of a Human Rights Committee. His Committee had been declared illegal following a banned march on the Ministry of the Interior, demanding news of political detainees.

Examiner's tips

The Examiner's tips found throughout the **Text commentary** and **Exam and coursework practice** sections highlight key points in the text, provide advice on avoiding common errors and offer useful hints on thoroughly preparing yourself for coursework and examination essays on this novel.

A word about pronunciation

Some words and names used in the story are Spanish and require a Spanish pronunciation. Note the pronunciation of the following:

Miguel – Me-gell (the 'g' is a hard 'g' as in go)
Juan – Whan
San Jose – San Ho-say
junta – hun-ta
Gemelos – he (short 'e')-me (short 'e')-los
Allende – Ay-yen-day

Text commentary

Chapter 1

It is the day before the spring general presidential elections in Chile. The Silver Lion is making an election speech to twenty thousand supporters in the stadium of Santiago. In his speech, the Silver Lion promises to curb the power of the military Junta that has been running the country. He promises democracy, justice, equality and freedom for all.

Juan Larreta's band, Los Obstinados, is going from the stadium in Santiago where they had played in support of the Alberti, to San José, the Silver Lion's home town and location of his final election speech. On their way they are shot at by the secret police. Guitarist Horacio Rivera is killed. Andres, Juan's only son, is thrown clear of the car and manages to hide from the police. The police drag Juan from the car and beat him. From his hiding place, Andres witnesses the burning of Horacio's body, Los Obstinados' instruments and the car, before it is pushed into the River Maipo. The secret police return to Santiago taking Juan as a prisoner.

Andres wants to get to San José as fast as possible to tell the Silver Lion of what has happened to his father and to warn Los Obstinados' drummer, Braulio, who was to meet them at the stadium. He manages to catch a lift with identical twins in an ancient van.

The twins, Isa and Beto, are puppeteers known as 'Marionetas De Los Gemelos'. They are on their way to San José hoping to do three shows for the crowds gathered to hear the Silver Lion. When they come across a road block, Beto gets out to investigate and learns that the Silver Lion has been shot dead at San José whilst making his speech. The Junta postpones the elections, declares a State of Emergency, enforces a curfew and blames the assassination on the Communists.

The twins and Andres return to Santiago. On the outskirts of Santiago they hear gunfire. The Junta is trying to suppress Resistance fighters. As the soldiers pass by, the twins and Andres narrowly miss being shot.

'We are once more winning the argument for democracy in this proud land...'

Freedom/ resistance

Miguel Alberti, know as 'the Silver Lion' because of his silver hair, is a philosopher and poet running for the presidency in Chile. The novel begins at the stadium of Santiago with the Silver Lion making a speech. He is a candidate for the people of Chile. He wishes to bring democracy to Chile. He says in his speech that recently Chile has been ruled by the army under an oppressive regime. He is a popular candidate as twenty thousand people come out to hear his speech. He refers to the people of Chile as 'Companeros', which is Spanish for companions. He encourages pride within his supporters by describing the country as 'this proud land'. He believes in justice, equality and freedom for all.

Alberti's popularity is a threat to the Junta, the armed military government, which has been running the country. The Junta is backed by the America government, and while it is in power the people of Chile suffer poor working conditions and poverty. The Junta is a totalitarian regime. (Totalitarian means a dictatorial one-party government.) If Alberti comes to power he will reduce the power of foreign governments over Chile's natural resources.

This novel presents the conflict between democracy and rule by force. Pay attention to details of each ideology as presented in this novel. Also keep track of which characters support which ideology. For more information see specimen exam question 2 on page 57.

'You, Larreta, will pay for your lies, and you'll suffer for your songs.'

Juan Larreta is a popular singer of political songs. His songs denounce brutal dictatorships and highlight human rights. He has cut short his tour of Peru to help the Silver Lion in his election campaign, and performs in the stadium that afternoon. Juan is known in Chile as 'the Minstrel of the People'. He performs in a trio called 'Los Obstinados', Spanish for 'the Obstinate Ones.' Like the Silver Lion, he poses a threat to the military and American-backed government and industries. Why are singers of political protest songs a threat to the American-backed government? Why do the trio call themselves Los Obstinados?

Brutality

Juan is travelling from the stadium with one of the other members of the trio – guitarist, Horacio Rivera – and his son, Andres, when they are shot at by Chile's secret police, the CNI. The shots force the old Chevrolet to swerve into a ditch. Horacio is killed instantly and Juan is dragged from the car by four soldiers. Andres is thrown clear. The secret police beat Juan, while Andres, in hiding, listens. The secret police know that a third passenger was in the car and they are looking for Andres. Why is it important for the CNI to find the third passenger?

Luckily they cannot find Andres. They set fire to the car and Horacio's body and push the burning vehicle into the River Maipo. The Security men punch and kick Juan into their car and head back to Santiago. Why is it important that the secret police dispose of all evidence?

How does this scene contrast with the opening scene? At first this scene is rather confusing to understand. Why has Watson chosen to present this scene in this way? The brutality in this scene foreshadows the force used by the Security and activities of the Junta.

Think about how the arrest of Juan Larreta would affect high ranking members of the Junta. See the specimen coursework question on page 60.

' ... but most of all his physique suggested staying-power and resilience.'

Andres Larreta is sixteen. His appearance is described in the opening chapter.

He looks frail, with a lanky and angular frame, bony shoulders, wide hips and protruding knees. His ungainly appearance is misleading, however, because his movement is lithe and balanced and agile. He is light on his feet. Most importantly he possesses stamina and resilience. These physical qualities will be crucial for his survival. What physical challenges does this quote suggest that Andres will encounter?

Andres

Prior to Andres' physical description, he had been contemplating whether escaping from the Security force was a brave and honourable act. He wonders if he would have been better off facing prison with his father. How can Andres' escape be of more use to his father?

When we first meet Andres he is in danger. There will be many more times in the novel when Andres faces danger. Think of the different types of danger, such as physical, psychological and political danger. What type of danger is Andres in? Think about the ways that Watson has made this episode exciting. For more detail see specimen exam question 1 on page 56.

'In Chile under the military Junta you trust the truth only with close friends.'

Notice the way Isa and Beto hesitated before picking up Andres. The Junta

is dangerous and innocent people can get hurt, arrested or just disappear for being caught with enemies of the regime. Andres' father has always disapproved of the Junta and tried to expose the truth about the its violations of human rights. Andres is also currently wanted by the Junta because he witnessed the murder of Horacio and the beating of Juan. Isa

Repression

and Beto know nothing about the stranger that they have picked up – he could be dangerous. Likewise, Andres knows nothing of the identical twins who are giving him a lift. They might support the Junta or even be spies. How will they be able to break the barrier of secrecy with one another and learn whether or not they can trust each other?

Narrative style and technique

Look closely at the style in which the last section of this chapter is written, starting after the final break. The book is written in the style of a political thriller. The action happens very quickly and is slightly confusing. This confusion helps to create the tense atmosphere. What is the effect of the following passage?

'For seconds only: they were too exposed. They scrambled. They ran. The gunfire became so deafening, so touchable, that it seemed to have thrown a wall around them, first barring their escape, then capsizing over them.'

The first half of the passage is written in short, simple sentences. Although the final sentence is long it is broken up into many phrases★, giving the same effect as short sentences. Why are short, simple sentences or phrases particularly suitable for conveying excitement and tension?

The opening chapter of any novel is extremely important because it sets the scene, sets the tone, introduces some of the main characters, starts the action, introduces a central conflict and introduces some of the main themes. When answering questions on it, be specific about the purposes achieved in this chapter.

A popular examination question concerns our expectations of characters following their introduction. Make detailed notes on your expectations of Andres, Isa, Beto and the Junta. When you have finished reading the novel, look over your notes on your initial expectations of these characters. How did each character's development match up with your expectations?

Chapter 2

Overnight the National Stadium in Santiago has been transformed into an interrogation centre. Hundreds of people have been taken prisoner and transported there by trucks.

Andres has a nightmare about his mother's suspicious death when he was nine years old, and wakes up to find himself in the mill where Isa and Beto live. He discovers that he was grazed by a bullet.

The Mercury newspaper reports the deaths of all the members of Los Obstinados, including Andres'. The story claims that Juan was a well-known alcoholic and that the accident was caused by his drunken driving. The report also says that Juan's popularity

★ A phrase is an element of a sentence normally containing more than one word, but lacking the subject–predicate structure of a clause.

has been declining since the death of his wife who had committed suicide. Andres is outraged by all of the lies in the report. Isa and Beto comfort Andres by telling him that they understand how he feels because their relatives have been missing for eighteen months.

The following day Andres sets out to tell the families and friends of Los Obstinados the truth about the car accident. Life in Santiago seems to be carrying on as usual until the Black Berets pursue and shoot a youth with long hair.

All of Juan's friends have been arrested and taken prisoner. Unfortunate prisoners go to the CNI's secret headquarters, the House of Laughter, for torture. The last time Juan was arrested and imprisoned, the persistence of friends and family brought about his release. This time Andres is alone in being able to help his father.

Andres goes to the National Stadium and sees Braulio being led off a truck with lots of other prisoners. On his way through the crowds to Braulio, he meets an American journalist, Don Chailey. The American is spotted taking photographs of the Junta's brutality. He gives Andres his camera, which could prove to be a valuable weapon.

'The gates of the National Stadium in Santiago have been opening and closing all through the night.'

It is the following day. Time is very important in this book. Note that the entire story takes place in the space of a week. Through the night the Junta has transformed the football stadium into an interrogation centre. Prisoners, such as Juan Larreta and resistance fighters, have been brought by the truckload to the stadium in the aftermath of Alberti's assassination. Who would the Junta be interested in arresting? Why?

Brutality

Narrative style and technique

From whose point of view is the story narrated? Are there any changes? Consider the perspective of the opening section of this chapter. What are the advantages of the third person point of view? The third person point of view can either be omniscient (which means that the narrator knows everything and sees everything, from *omni* meaning all and *scientia* meaning knowledge) or limited (which means that the narrator can only report what happens, but not a character's motivations for his/her actions). The omniscient point of view is used in the opening of this chapter, allowing us to hear the author's voice. Sometimes the story is told from Andres' point of view. This is called the first person point of view. Keep track of when we hear Watson's voice and when we hear Andres' voice.

'The killer squads who had been threatening Juan with his own death if he continued to sing songs attacking the rich, attacking the generals for their tyranny?'

Early in this chapter we learn some details of Andres' background. He remembers his mother's death when he was nine years old. It appears that she

Andres

was hit by a car, but Andres saw a man in the moving car aiming a pistol at his mother. Andres and his father suspected that she was murdered by a killer squad in revenge for Juan's songs of political protest. This event is linked to the threat the soldier gives Juan in Chapter 1. Why would Juan sing songs that attack the rich and the generals for their tyranny? How are the rich connected to the generals? Think about all the reasons why Andres would be recalling his mother's suspicious death now.

We glean a lot of information about the societal structure of Chile in this chapter as Andres walks through Santiago. Make notes on the different societal groups and which political ideology they support. For more information see question 2 of the example exam questions on page 57.

'You're among friends'

The action and danger of the preceding night has confirmed that Beto and

Triumph of the human spirit

Isa can trust Andres. Trust and loyalty are crucial to the Resistance from the state terrorism of the Junta. This is the beginning of an important relationship between the three young people. Their trust and support of each other will be contrasted throughout the rest of story with the lack of trust, lies and uncertainty of the oppressive military state they are now living under. Why is it significant that Isa says the above statement to Andres?

Isa and Beto have also read about Andres' true identity from the report in *The Mercury* of Andres' supposed death. Isa and Beto know what it is to have one's family disappear. Their parents, uncle and cousin disappeared eighteen months ago without a trace. Isa and Beto suspect that the Junta is behind their relatives' disappearance. The three young people are alone in the world without family – they only have each other to rely on.

'After a while, you come to hate talking in whispers.'

Isa

Isa has made a puppet in the image of General Zuckerman. She calls the puppet 'General Zuckero'. What would be the penalty if the Junta caught her poking fun or, even more seriously, exposing the truth through the puppet General Zuckero?

Isa is tired of being suppressed by fear. Her reluctance to 'talk in whispers' for fear of being found out by the Junta, is a small step towards the Resistance movement needed by the people to liberate themselves from the Junta's oppression and brutality.

Isa is a brave girl with a lot of pluck and a good sense of humour. She also has a strong sense of right and wrong. She knows what the Junta is doing is wrong, and she also thinks that it is wrong not to fight back in any way you can. In this scene she has made Andres laugh and has impressed him with her brave spirit. Pay attention to their growing feelings for one another.

Freedom/ resistance

'The words cheered Andres; they sharpened his purpose. I'm not alone.'

As Andres is passing through the city, he notices that life is carrying on as usual.

The only difference is that people today 'are talking in whispers'. He is reminded of a song about 'talking in whispers/eyes on the ground' by Chico Buarque. The song gives Andres a sense of hope as he realises that his people have suffered this situation before and survived. The song inspires stronger feelings of resistance in him. What do the words to this song mean? Keep notes on all of the poems, songs and stories Andres thinks of to raise his spirits.

Andres

Note that the main street in Santiago is called Avenida Bernardo O'Higgins, better known as the Alameda. Bernardo O'Higgins liberated Chile from Spain. Why is it ironic that life is carrying on as if nothing has happened on the street named after a freedom fighter?

'The youth was hit in the middle of the back.'

The shooting of the youth with the long hair by the Black Berets is further confirmation for Andres' of the Junta's brutality. He wonders if the youth's only crime was to have long hair. This incident prepares us for the increasing incidences of brutality throughout this chapter.

Brutality

Following this incident Andres discovers that the homes of Horacio, Braulio and Juan's friends' families have been visited by the Black Berets. The men have been arrested and taken prisoner. Braulio's home has been ransacked. Andres senses that many of the woman are frightened to talk to him. Why are they frightened?

Notice that Horacio, Braulio and Juan's friends all live in poor areas of Santiago. Meanwhile the wealthy on the Alameda fly national flags celebrating the Junta's victory. Why are the enemies of the Junta the poor and their supporters the rich?

> ' "And if he's not lucky?"
> The caretaker drew a finger-blade across his throat. "Then it'll
> be the House of Laughter, God keep him!" '

The caretaker at Juan's music publisher mentions the secret headquarters of the CNI, sarcastically referred to as 'the House of Laughter'. This is where unlucky prisoners are tortured into divulging important information about the activities of the Resistance movement. Andres cannot understand why the Junta would want to torture his father as he would have no useful information for them. This interchange foreshadows Andres' experience at the House of Laughter.

'What's in this camera might be just as valuable as bullets.'

**Freedom/
resistance**

Don Chailey photographed the beating of Braulio. The American readily agreed with Andres that 'The world's got to know what's happening here'. Andres knows that the photographs are definite evidence of the Junta's violation of human rights. How could the pictures of Braulio's beating be more valuable to the Resistance movement than bullets? Don Chailey had come to Chile to cover the elections. What other incidents may Chailey have photographed?

Again Andres is in a dangerous situation at the end of this chapter. Define which type of danger he is in and look carefully at how Watson has presented this episode. For more detail see question 1 of the example exam questions on page 56.

Every chapter presents key events which are pivotal to the development of the story. For instance, Andres' acquiring of Don Chailey's camera will prove indispensable to the resolution of the story. Make notes on what you think the other key events in these opening chapters are. Keep track of how these key events influence other events throughout the rest of the novel. Examiner's expect you know how these key events are initiated, developed and resolved. It is also a good idea to note key lines in the text which illustrate the key events.

Chapter 3

Before returning to the mill, Andres visits Juan's house. The Black Berets are there. They burn books and manuscripts, declare Juan Larreta an enemy of the state and ban his music. Andres restrains his anger, but an Indian man who protests is arrested and bundled into the army van.

Andres returns to the mill. He tells the twins about the camera. The three go to Diego Rosales' printshop. Diego's printshop has been visited by the Junta. Luckily they missed his darkroom, so Diego can develop the prints. The photographs prove that the Junta assassinated the Silver Lion.

Diego's printing press is hidden in pieces around the city. He has a plan for reassembling all of the parts of his printing press and printing leaflets advertising the Junta's brutality to the rest of the world. He warns the three youngsters, though, that it is very dangerous to join the Resistance movement, and that once they become involved there is no turning back. Andres and the twins are keen to get involved.

'And the books were shovelled towards the bonfire.'

Juan and Andres' book collections are burned. Why are the soldiers ordered to burn books in the street?

'The scene before him of vicious and insane destruction was no laughing matter.'

Repression

The Junta refers to Juan as 'an enemy of the state'. The Interior Ministry has banned the publication of his works and the performance of his songs. Under the Junta's rule there is no freedom of speech. This is a violation of the 19th Article of The Universal Declaration of Human Rights, the right to freedom of opinion. What are consequences of a state where individuals are not allowed to have opinions differing from the government's?

'He had listened to lies and he had not responded. He had not even whispered a protest.'

Andres

Andres watches his father's books and songs being burned. He hears his father declared an enemy of the state and his music banned. He notices that the officer who made the declaration waited 'as though half-expecting a backlash of protest'. No protest is voiced audibly, but Andres and many others must be protesting in their hearts. Andres knows that not only would it be dangerous for him to protest at this time, but he has a secret weapon, namely Don Chailey's camera containing the photographs. Although it hurts to see his father treated like this, it will be far more effective to wait until the time is right to get the photographs printed and distribute them. What happens to the Indian who does protest?

'... they say he's a member of the old Resistance.'

Diego Rosales

Diego Rosales is Horacio's cousin. He owns a printshop. Andres trusts Diego to help them print Don Chailey's photographs because Diego was a member of the old Resistance movement during the military coup following the assassination of Salvador Allende on the 11th of September,

1973. Diego prints leaflets. In what way can this help Juan, Braulio and Don Chailey?

Remember to add Diego to your notes about the characters who support democracy. What qualities does Diego possess that are desirable for democratic supporters in this novel? For more information see question 2 of the example exam questions on page 57.

'Beto grinned. He put on the drawl of an American movie cop: "We want a slice of the action, Man." '

Beto

Beto is the joker of the group. By nature he is light-hearted and prefers making jokes to taking things seriously. He is happy for Isa to dominate the relationship. Isa always knows what she is doing, but sometimes Beto just goes along for the thrill, not really aware of the true danger involved. Contrast his attitude in this scene to Isa's.

Beto is also sensitive and cannot hide his emotions. When did we see this side of Beto in Chapter 2?

'Just occasionally fate deals you a little bit of luck.'

Freedom/
resistance

Diego is referring to the fact that the Junta did not go into his Ladies' room and therefore missed discovering his darkroom. This stroke of luck, coupled with Andres' good fortune of being given Don Chailey's camera, will allow them to develop the pictures of the Junta's brutality. In fact, fate has dealt the three youngsters quite a bit of good luck so far. List all the examples of Isa, Beto and Andres' good fortune that you can think of.

'Long live the Resistance!'

Diego Rosales typifies the spirit of the Resistance. He was crippled during the last Resistance movement as a result of torture. He was also imprisoned. Despite walking 'achingly up the basement steps', he welcomes the three youngsters and immediately makes light of the grave situation that they face. His love of jokes and hopeful outlook proves that physical torture may break bones, but it cannot break a man's spirit. Describe his reaction to the possibilities presented by the camera.

Rosales is also an experienced Resistance soldier. He suspected the election was a fake, planned by General Zuckerman to sniff out democratic sympathisers. He was wise to hide his printing press in anticipation.

'We've got something here that could rock Zuckerman and the Junta back on their Nazi heels.'

Diego is amazed by the evidence of the Junta's brutality and political crimes as captured in Don Chailey's photographs. The reference to

General Zuckerman

the Nazis is fitting. The Nazis were ruled by a dictator, Hitler, as the Junta is led by another dictator, General Zuckerman. The Nazis ruled by force, murdered thousands of innocent Jews and repressed anyone who opposed them. It was very dangerous for people such as Shindler to help them. Likewise, the Junta rules by military force and is responsible for the deaths for hundreds of innocent Chileans. As we have seen in this chapter, it is very dangerous to be a part of the Resistance movement. Like the Nazis in Germany, the Junta has control of the media and delivers only pro-Junta propaganda. Diego mentions Nazi heels as a reference to the boots worn by the military soldiers in both regimes.

'So the Junta puts the blame on the Communists ... Which gives them the excuse to, to ... '

Don Chailey's series of photographs of the Security man with a walkie-talkie

Repression

and revolver confirm that the Junta was responsible for the assassination of the Silver Lion. The Junta, however, has blamed the Communists. Andres realises that by publicly blaming the Communists the Junta has the perfect excuse to search homes and arrest suspected Communists. The public who supported the Silver Lion's call for democracy would condone the arrest of Communists as they would be viewed as the true enemies of democracy and not the Junta.

'I mean, if these pictures got on to the front pages of the world's press!'

Freedom/
resistance

Diego knows from experience that the best way to fight the Junta is to alert the rest of the world to their human rights violations and political crimes. If these pictures were published, many governments around the world would denounce the actions of the Junta and they would be watched closely by the United Nations. If Diego can assemble all of the parts of his printing press, he can print the photographs for distribution.

So far only three days have passed. Much of Chapter 2 and all of Chapter 3 take place on the third day. Make a list of all of the important plot developments which have taken place on this third day.

Narrative style
and technique

Examiners reward candidates who are aware of alternative perspectives in texts and can compare these perspectives in writing. Juan Larreta is revered by many and loathed by others. Which sectors of the society see Juan Larreta as an enemy of the state? Why? Which sectors of the society see Juan Larreta as a hero? Why?

■ Self-test Questions Chapters 1–3

Uncover the plot

Delete two of the three alternatives given to find the correct plot. Beware possible misconceptions and muddles.

The story opens the day/month/week before the presidential elections in Argentina/Chile/Ecuador. Ten/twenty/thirty thousand people have come to the Coliseum/main square/Stadium of Buenos Aires/Quito/Santiago to hear the election speech of Miguel Alberti, affectionately known as the Golden Hog/Minstrel of the People/Silver Lion. The popular duet/trio/group Los Obstinados play at the proceedings. On their way to San Francisco/San Jose/Santa Fe the duet/trio/group's car is shot at by the Black/Green/Red Berets. Braulio/Horacio/Romeo is killed. Andres Larreta is thrown clear but watches his father, Antonio/Juan/Joaquin, being beaten by the soldiers. Andres/Braulio/Horacio gets a lift to San Francisco/San Jose/Santa Fe in a car/lorry/van with the twins Eva/Isa/Maria and Alpha/Beto/Carlos. The twins are acrobats/dancers/puppeteers. At a road block they learn that Miguel Alberti/Juan Larreta/General Zuckerman has been shot while making his final election speech in San Francisco/San Jose/Santiago. The Democrats/Junta/Socialists take(s) control of the situation and impose(s) a ban/curfew/tax. The Junta blames the assassination on the Communists/Liberals/Tories. Beto, Isa and Andres return to Port of Spain/Santiago/Willemstad. On the outskirts of Santiago they hear gunfire/music/thunder. They abandon the car/lorry/van while the tanks and soldiers pass.

The next day the National Stadium has been turned into a hospital/an interrogation centre/the headquarters of the Resistance. Andres/Beto/Isa has a nightmare about the death of his brother/mother/sister. The *Mercury/Sun/Times* newspaper reports that Juan and Andres/Beto/Isa were killed in the car accident. The Security know that Andres/Horacio/Miguel is still alive. The next day/week/month Andres visits the homes of the friends and families of the Junta/Los Obstinados/Marionetas de los Gemelos. On his way he sees a dog/woman/youth shot dead by the Black/Green/Red Berets. He also learns that the homes of Juan's friends have been visited by the Church/CNI/Resistance and thechildren/men/women have been arrested. Andres/Beto/Jose returns to the car/mill/stadium and sees Braulio/Isa/Juan. Andres meets anAmerican/Australian/English journalist who gives his camera/gun/money to Andres when he is spotted taking photographs by the Americans/Black Berets/Resistance.

Against the advice of Beto/Father Mariano/Isa, Andres returns to his house. The Black/Green/Red Berets burn/ransack/rob the house and burn/confiscate/steal

Andres'/Horacio's/Juan's possessions. An officer declares Andres/Juan/the Silver Lion a(n) enemy/friend/prisoner of the state. An Indian man who cheers/laughs/protests is bundled into an army van. Andres returns to the mill/stadium/van and tells Isa and Beto about the camera/car/printing press. He manages to save a guitar/leaflet/picture from Juan's house. On the leaflet is the address/name/phone number of Horacio's cousin, Diego, who owns a betting/print/sweets shop. The three visit Diego after curfew/hours/midnight. Although his shop has been ransacked, the Communists/CNI/Resistance found nothing, as they missed his darkroom/money/printing press. Diego develops/prints/sells the photos. They contain evidence that the Communists/Democrats/Junta assassinated Miguel Alberti/General Zuckerman/Juan Larreta. The three are keen to help the Communist/Junta/Resistance movement, but Diego warns them that it is very dangerous/expensive/tiring.

Who? What? Why? When? Where? How?

1 Where is the Silver Lion shot dead?
2 Who is the people's choice for president?
3 What does Andres think Isa looks like?
4 Why does Beto nickname Andres 'Towny'?
5 What did Juan nickname his wife?
6 Why did the Junta miss Diego's darkroom?
7 Why is a curfew imposed?
8 How is Andres' strength encouraged by the Araucanian Indian?
9 Why does the Junta blame the Communists for Alberti's murder?
10 Where does Isa work?

Who says that, and to whom?

1 'Any more heroes?'
2 'Sisters are born bullies.'
3 ' ... it looks as though we've given bed and board to a real barrel of trouble.'
4 'Nothing to do with me ... I missed my bus to San Jose.'
5 'After curfew, troops are shooting on sight.'
6 'You murderers!'
7 'He's the cat with nine lives ... '
8 'Let us therefore stand together, in unity, against the enemy within.'
9 'People who live such quiet lives that the CNI don't know they exist.'
10 'Take this – I'm finished.'

Open quotes

Identify the scene; complete the phrase or exchange; identify the speaker and the character being spoken to.

1 ' ... send the solders back to their barracks – ...'
2 'For just seeing these pictures...'
3 'Of course the Security too were at the graveside:...'
4 'You want to help? Okay, but understand this – ...'
5 ' ... am I really doing this for Dad, for glory...'
6 'He must have been crazy, taking such risks. And for what? For glory?' 'For...'
7 'We checked your brain...'
8 'Brothers take running jumps at things – ...'
9 ' ... people were relieved – sometimes eager – ...'
10 'All you'll be needing is a cool head, lots of luck – and...'

Chapter 4

The Junta's reign of terror continues. Lorry loads of prisoners are brought to the stadium by the hour. On arrival, the prisoners are routinely beaten.

At Santiago's Central Station, meanwhile, Diego's plan to recover all the individual parts of his printing press is in full swing. Despite a few close calls, Andres, Isa and Beto are successful in getting all of the parts of the press together.

They are followed when they leave the station. To save the press, Beto drives out of the town and drops Andres off in some fir woods with the parts of the press. Beto and Isa return to town and avoid arrest by performing a puppet show in a crowded school playground.

In the woods, Andres falls into a quarry and knocks himself unconscious. When he comes to, he buries the sacks containing the printing press in the quarry. Just as he is climbing out of the quarry he hears trucks. The army is bringing prisoners to the quarry. Andres witnesses the CNI shooting the prisoners.

Narrative style and technique

Consider the ending of the previous chapter. We are hopeful because Diego has a plan to get his printing press assembled. He has also warned Andres, Isa and Beto about the danger of joining the Resistance movement. This chapter opens with a vivid description of the Junta's brutality towards the Resistance. How does this contrast create tension?

'The prisoners face death as sudden as a precipice.'

Watson describes what he sarcastically calls the prisoners' 'official welcome'.

Brutality

Keep track of the Junta's brutal and repressive methods throughout the book. For instance, in Chapter 1 it imposes the curfew to make secret meetings between members of the Resistance movement difficult. In Chapter 2 the Black Berets shoot the youth with the long hair. After you have compiled your log, consider how the acts of brutality are becoming more severe. Compare the beating of Juan in Chapter 1 to the beating of Braulio at the end of Chapter 2 and to the beatings which open this chapter.

'It's on. Friday. Prompt at twelve.'

Outline Diego's plan in detail. Keep track of the individual parts that Andres, Isa and Beto play. Notice that Isa now wears the Silver Lion's green panama hat. Reread the opening of Chapter 1 to remind yourself how it came to be in her possession.

Freedom/ resistance

The execution of the plan is very tense. How does Watson create tension in the following excerpt: 'Andres bit his lip: he's going to move her on.'?

Firstly, Watson makes the scene visually tense. Andres is biting his lip. The police have been watching Isa and one of them is crossing the forecourt towards her. Secondly, think about the dual perspective presented in this passage. Watson switches from a third person point of view, to Andres' point of view. How is this dual point of view effective in creating suspense?

As in Chapter 1, the presentation of events is confusing. Why has Watson deliberately done this? Think how tension is created visually and audibly.

Watson has also included touches of humour into the scene, such as the irony of Andres falling into the old woman's paper as she is trying to read General Zuckerman's speech. How do the touches of humour heighten the build up of tension?

Consider how tension is created in the following passages:

'The rear doors of the van open. Three plain-clothes men descend. At the same moment, the officer of the Black Berets strides out through the gate of platform nine. Two policemen follow him, escorting the girls Andres helped only minutes ago.'

'He looks right and left. He does not see Andres. He turns right. He walks a few paces. He stops. he changes course, brooding, getting angry.'

'Beto brakes hard. The doors open. Isa is out, helping with the parcels. "Well done, Towny!" cries Beto.

"I think I'm being followed." '

Later in this chapter, when Andres separates from Isa and Beto, the narrative is broken into two. Watson shifts between Isa and Beto in the city and Andres in the woods. Why has Watson split the narrative? What effect does this create?

'Isa stayed calm.'

The strength of Isa's character is further developed in this chapter. She appears to stay much calmer than Andres during the execution of the plan at the train station. Being calm and focused is crucial to Isa's role in the plan. Policemen are watching her and any sign of nervousness would arouse their suspicions.

When they make their getaway from the station Andres and Beto relax, but Isa keeps watch out of the rear-view mirror and notices that they are being followed. Beto and Andres are unnerved by their pursuers and it is Isa that they both look to for direction. Isa is a natural leader, knows exactly what to do and gives the orders.

After dropping off Andres and the printing press, it is Isa's nimble mind that thinks of going to a school just as the children are coming out to put off their followers. Not only is she clever and emotionally strong, she is also beautiful. How do we know that Andres is definitely starting to fall in love with her?

Setting is crucial to the impact of a novel because it creates the important physical dimension of a story which arouses our interest by heightening our senses. It is likely to come up in exam questions. In this chapter Watson plausibly creates the atmosphere of a train station. Pay attention to the precise details which bring the train station alive. Now explore the other settings presented so far in this novel. What do these setting add to our understanding of the political conflict presented in the novel? Keep using this same approach to setting as you read and prepare the remainder of this novel for examination revision. Finally, remember that weather and temperature is part of the setting. Pay particular attention to any details of weather conditions.

Chapter 5

Andres waits until the soldiers leave and then searches the bodies of the dead to see if Juan is among them. He comes across Don Chailey's body. Andres will inform the families of the other victims he has been able to identify.

Meanwhile, Isa and Beto finish their puppet show. Their followers leave them to join in a gun battle against Resistance fighters. Isa fears that the escaped ring-leaders of the Resistance will go to Father Mariano's seminary, where she advised Andres to go.

Andres takes refuge at the Seminary of Our Lady of Mercy. Although Father Mariano has been ordered to co-operate with the Junta, and deny assistance to enemies of the state, he allows Andres to stay the night. Ignorant of the gun battle that day, Andres watches as a wounded Resistance soldier is brought in. The soldier is Hernando Salas, the most wanted man in Santiago. Andres also sees a doctor arrive. He falls back asleep for a few hours but is abruptly woken by the CNI. He hears Father Mariano and Sister Theresa being beaten. Terrified, he escapes from the seminary only to find himself face to face with four armed Black Berets.

'Andres spoke out loud: "Adios, little boy!" '

So far we have seen many facets of Andres' personality. We see his reckless

Andres

side, when he returns to Juan's house, his masculine side, when he tries to impress Isa, his sensitive side, when he thinks about his mother, his dutiful side, when he visits Juan's friends, and his adventurous side, when he hides the printing press alone in the woods. In this chapter we see Andres grow up. He is aware that checking the dead bodies in the quarry is a manly act and he audibly bids the child inside him goodbye. It is not an easy decision for him and he has to talk himself into it. What two voices inside Andres grapple with the prospect of inspecting the dead bodies?

Narrative style and technique

Look at the narrative style of the opening of this chapter. As we have seen before, we have two perspectives narrating

Andres' experience. One perspective is the third person, author-narrator, and the other is Andres' first hand account. Make sure that you can distinguish between Andres' voice and the author's voice.

Reread the paragraph which begins: 'Andres watched the soldiers climb aboard the trucks. He felt freezing cold, as though his blood had been drained from him...'. Whose perspective is this? Look at how each sentence starts: *Andres watched..., He felt..., He watched..., He was not..., Yet he did not..., He was..., He saw..., He saw..., He saw....*What is the effect of repeating this sentence structure?

'Not knowing – that is the most painful thing in the world.'

One of the worst consequences of this political situation is that people

Freedom/
resistance

disappear and are never heard of again. Families wait day after day for some word to confirm whether their loved one is dead or alive. For many people it is a relief to hear that the missing relative is dead, because at least then they can start to come to terms with the loss. When the person is missing, however, it is natural to want to do all one can to help find them, but governments such as General Zuckerman's make it almost impossible to trace the person, let alone help them. Andres and the twins have all been in this terrible state of uncertainty about relatives. This is the reason why all three have joined the Resistance movement.

'Andres put down his spoon. He was tired and ready to take offence.'

In this scene, where Andres and Father Mariano sit down to eat at the

Andres

seminary, we witness Andres' temper. He takes offence at Father Mariano's remark about one of Juan's songs which mocks the Church. How does Father Mariano quell the tense atmosphere?

This scene provides a realistic development in the presentation of Andres' character. His bravery and strong resolve in the previous scene are contrasted by his quick temper and defensiveness in this scene. It is understandable and natural that Andres is easily irked after his exhausting day and the horror of what he has witnessed. We have, however, seen Andres suppress his anger at the slandering of Juan's name in previous chapters. Why is he unable to suppress his indignation with Father Mariano?

Clearly Andres and Father Mariano have not hit it off. Andres is disappointed that the priest does not ask him to tell his story. When Father Mariano explains that he has been instructed by the Archbishop to co-operate with the Junta and deny all help to enemies of the state, Andres becomes defensive again. What bad thought does Andres have about the priest later in this chapter?

'He was intrigued: how many reasons did she weigh in the balance before she agreed to break curfew, risk arrest and torture, to bring comfort to a wounded stranger – a wanted man?'

Andres is inspired by the woman doctor who comes out in the middle of the

Triumph of the human spirit

night to attend to the wounded Resistance soldier. It is highly dangerous, and the doctor is risking her own life. The wounded soldier, however, is a human being and the doctor's respect of human life overrides any personal fear. In most dire situations there are people who risk personal danger to do what they think is right. The fact that the soldier is a stranger to the doctor, suggests the doctor has a generous spirit. As Andres drifts off to sleep, he thinks his mother and Isa would have shown the same courage, generosity and righteousness.

Narrative style and technique

Look closely at the closing scene in which Andres escapes from the seminary. As in the closing of Chapter 1, this scene is written in the style of the political thriller. Pay particular attention to the way in which a feeling of distance, as in moving away from the seminary, is achieved. What is the effect of the following passage?

'The seminary wall was well behind him. Another near miss. Another closed chapter. He felt pain and a candleflame of elation. Then: "Halt!"'

The most striking feature of this passage is the contrast between Andres' feelings of relief and then the sudden capture. The soldier's voice is unexpected and literally comes out of the dark. Irony is created through this contrast. Just as Andres was thinking he was safe, and that the danger of the seminary is behind him, he is captured. This is merely the beginning of his troubles and he is in serious danger. How is the feeling of surprise and the halting of movement reinforced in the writing style?

Again Andres is in grave danger. Define the type of danger and add your notes from the textual comment above. For more detail see question 1 of the example exam questions on page 56.

Andres' visit to the Seminary of Our Lady of Mercy introduces the religious side of Chilean culture. The Catholic religion is central to Chilean culture and society. Examiners will expect you to be familiar with the social, historical and cultural context of the novel. Look back through the early chapters for any earlier references to the Church or religion, or any other aspects of Chilean society and culture. Continue to keep track of any social, historical or cultural references as you read and prepare the remaining chapters for coursework and examination revision.

Chapter 6

The Junta's search for the Resistance leaders continues. Isa wakes up in the early hours of Saturday morning, fearing that Andres is in trouble. She wants go straight to the seminary despite the curfew, but Beto sensibly talks her out of such foolishness.

Meanwhile, Andres is taken to the House of Laughter. He is taken to a long dark room. A hood is put over his head and his wrists are handcuffed. During the questioning he is shaken, slapped, beaten, kicked and hung up by his wrists. His answers are not helpful to his interrogators and he is set to be tortured with water and wires.

Isa visits the seminary alone. Father Mariano has been taken for questioning. Sister Theresa gives Andres' package of the mementoes of the massacred prisoners to Isa. Sister Theresa fears Father Mariano will not survive torture because he has a heart condition. Isa is hopeful that between Don Chailey's photographs and the mementoes she has enough evidence to expose the truth about the Junta.

'You and me are switching characters.'

Isa

Beto

Up until this chapter, we have seen Isa as the more level headed and sensible of the twins. In this scene we see Isa acting irrationally and Beto being the calm, practical one, talking her out of doing something foolish. Why is it realistic that Beto and Isa would sometimes switch characters in their relationship? What is the effect of presenting each twin during moments of strength and weakness?

In terms of characterisation, it is more realistic and interesting to have characters show many sides to their personalities. Watson creates depth to Isa's character by giving her a moment of weakness.

'I guess you must be in love.'

Isa

Isa is uncharacteristically impetuous for two reasons. Firstly, she has woken up out of a nightmare about Andres and she is naturally upset. Secondly, she is in love with Andres and understandably wants to know as soon as possible if he is in danger.

How does Isa grow as a character now that she is in love with Andres?

'There had been too many other prisoners for Andres to get a beating-up all to himself.'

As in Chapter 4, Watson injects humour into the narrative. In Chapter 4 much of the humour is visual. In this example, the humour is created through

Narrative style and technique

sarcasm. Sarcasm is the use of bitter or obviously ironic language. Here the tone of the statement is sarcastic. Why is sarcasm effective in presenting the absurdity of the Junta's actions? Keep track of all the subtle uses of humour throughout this chapter.

'Fix Isa's smile over the goalposts of your brain.'

Andres is falling in love with Isa. He tries to keep his spirits up by thinking

Triumph of the human spirit

about her rather than the impending danger facing him. Love is a strong emotion and can give people the emotional strength to survive terrible circumstances. Notice that in the beginning of the story, Andres gathered strength from thinking about his father. Now he is turning to thoughts of Isa, in addition to his father, for emotional strength. Keep track of how Andres' love for Isa helps him survive throughout the rest of the novel.

'The voice of the first interrogator was calm, in monotone, difficult to locate...'
'This second voice was high-pitched, irritated, full of bad temper and impatience. Two voices, then. Andres named them – the Snake and the Hog.'

A hood is slipped over Andres' head so that he cannot identify his

Snake and Hog

interrogators. This is the headquarters of the secret police and they do not want their identities revealed. Andres distinguishes between the two interrogators immediately. How can he tell that the Snake is the more senior of the two? The Snake is the calm one and the Hog is the bad tempered one who does most of the physical beating. Andres' nicknames for the two are examples of Watson's subtle use of humour in this chapter.

Why are the nicknames suitable to the personalities of the two men? Which do you think is the more threatening of the two?

Pay particular attention to the characterisation of the two torturers. Think about how this episode would be different if it were narrated from the Snake's point of view. See the specimen coursework question on page 60.

'The only privilege granted to you is to breathe. It is a privilege we shall honour only so long as it suits our purposes. Do you understand?'

The Snake begins his reign of brutality by verbally threatening Andres. During

Brutality

the questioning Andres is physically beaten every time the Snake and Hog think he is being deliberately uncooperative. In the course of the questioning, Andres is shaken, smacked, kicked, and punched. His nose is broken. To increase his pain he is hung up to force the weight of his body onto his broken and bruised joints. When the hanging fails to break Andres, they resort to electric shock torture.

'Andres knew he could not go on lying, not from this point. All he could do was omit what information might be vital. What did they know?'

Naturally Andres cannot tell them the truth, but he becomes tangled within

Andres

his own lies. When he realises that he cannot carry on lying, he recalls advice that Juan must have given him about being interrogated. Later on in the chapter, when he is hung up, he remembers the advice that 'Talking… keeps their fists away.' Andres is extraordinarily strong to withstand the beating and torture to which he is subjected.

Narrative style and technique

Andres' interrogation and torture are realistically horrific. One way in which Watson achieves this is by presenting the scene from Andres' perspective, inside the hood. We cannot see what is going on, so Andres has to describe his suffering through what he hears and feels. The suffocating and uncomfortable atmosphere Andres experiences inside the hood heighten our discomfort in reading this scene. Describe the effect of the following description:

'Andres was choking on his blood. He could not staunch the bleeding from his nose because his arms were fastened behind him. He tried to tilt his head back, but the Hog had him by the hood and the hair.'

Whether the narrative is told in the first person or in the third person, the focus is on Andres' feelings, not the interrogators.

Compare the first scene of Andres' interrogation to the final scene of the chapter. How is the second scene made more intense? Why is it effective that the narrative is broken up into two scenes separated by Isa's visit to Sister Theresa, rather than one long scene? Why is the ending of this scene particularly effective?

Examiners like candidates to be aware of how writers prepare readers for certain events. Watson has skilfully prepared us for Andres' arrest and torture since the beginning of the novel. Firstly, in the opening chapter, Juan Larreta is arrested and taken away. So far we have no idea of what has happened to him or whether he is still alive. In the second chapter we see the rise of the Junta's brutality when they shoot the youth with long hair and when they beat Braulio at the stadium. In the third chapter we meet Diego Rosales who is a survivor of the Junta's torture during a previous military coup. Keep a flowchart of these events and any others that you can think of that have foreshadowed Andres' torture.

■ Self-test Questions Chapters 4–6

Uncover the plot
Delete two of the three alternatives given to find the correct plot. Beware possible misconceptions and muddles.

There are six hundred/thousand/million prisoners at the stadium and more are brought every minute/hour/day. Andres and the twins carry out Diego's/General Zuckerman's/Juan's plan on Friday at the Santiago airport/coach terminal/train station. Andres is dressed up as a conductor/porter/soldier. Diego's friends leave parts of the camera/printing press/tape recorder in the lockers/ticket office/toilets and drop the combination/envelopes/keys into Andres'/Beto's/Isa's case/hand/panama. Andres retrieves the combinations/envelopes/keys, collects the items from the lockers/ticket office/toilets and wheels them on a trolley to the car/lorry/van. Andres and the twins successfully collect all the parts of the camera/printing press/tape recorder and drive away. They are arrested/followed/searched, so they head out of town. Andres is dropped off with the sacks and he hides them in a cave/quarry/tree. The twins lose their admirers/followers/friends at a church/hospital/school. Andres sees prisoners beaten/shot/stabbed at the quarry/stadium/station. He checks the bodies to see if Braulio/Diego/Juan is among them. Don Chailey/Jack Normanton/Diego Rosales is among the dead. Andres finds the journalist's camera/press card/wallet. Andres will try to contact the families of the men he could identify/recognise/see.

There is a four-/five-/six-hour gun battle between the Security and the Black Berets/Communists/Resistance. The ring-leaders of the Communists/Junta/Resistance died/escaped/surrendered. Beto/Isa/Rosa worries that the escaped ring-leaders will go to Father Mariano's church/house/seminary to hide. Andres goes to the church/house/seminary for the night because he does not have time to get back to the car/mill/van before curfew/midnight/sunset. Against the orders of the Archbishop/Junta/Pope, Father Mariano lets Andres stay. During the night, a wounded Communist/Resistance/Security soldier is brought in followed by a doctor/nurse/policeman. Later the Communists/Security/Resistance arrive and beat up Andres/Father Mariano/Hernando Salas. Andres escapes from the church/house/seminary, only to be captured by the Black/Green/Red Berets.

Helen/Isa/Theresa has a nightmare about Andres/Beto/Father Mariano. She tries to visit the printshop/seminary/stadium straight away, but Andres/Beto/Braulio makes her see sense about the danger of going out during the curfew/dark/

wee hours. Andres is taken to the House of Laughter/quarry/Stadium. A blindfold/hat/hood is put over his head so that he cannot identify his captors/guards/interrogators. He nicknames his captors/guards/interrogators Hog and Rat/Snake/Weasel. He is badly beaten and his arm/knee/nose is broken. He does not give his captors/guards/interrogators any useful information so they prepare to beat/kill/torture him with electric shocks/stretching/suffocating treatment. Later in the day, Isa visits the printshop/seminary/stadium. Sister Theresa has a broken arm/knee/nose and bad bruising. The doctor/Hernando Salas/Father Mariano has been taken away for medical help/prayer/questioning and Sister Theresa fears he will die if tortured because of his arthritis/heart condition/haemophilia. She tells Isa that Andres/Beto/Hernando Salas was there the night before but not in the morning. She hopes that he escaped/vanished/was arrested. She gives Isa a(n) address/package/photo that Andres had left. She relates Andres'/Hernando Salas'/Father Mariano's story about the shooting of Braulio/Don Chailey/Juan Larreta. Isa knows that this is irrelevant/silly/valuable information.

Who? What? Why? When? Where? How?

1 What false name does Andres give his interrogators?
2 Who is Hernando Salas?
3 What day of the week is the plan to retrieve the printer carried out?
4 Where does Andres hide the sacks containing the printing press?
5 How will Andres be tortured?
6 Why do the Security beat Father Mariano and Sister Theresa?
7 Who does Andres discover among the dead at the quarry?
8 What does Andres witness at the quarry?
9 When did Isa first want to visit the seminary?
10 Why didn't Isa tell Beto that a second set of Don Chailey's prints were in the van?

Who says that, and to whom?

1 'Hey… Andres doesn't need help from panickers.'
2 'That's why I think I gave Andres the world's worst, stupidest advice.'
3 'You oaf!'
4 'Any more of this and I'll need a heart transplant.'
5 'Talking, that keeps their fists away.'
6 'The less we know of your business, Andres, the better.'
7 'Do not move, boy!'
8 'Saved by the bell!'
9 'The Constitution does not extend to this place.'
10 'Over the years we've got rather good at hiding things.'

Open quotes

Identify the scene; complete the phrase; identify the speaker and the character being spoken to.

1 'Under the front seat of the van, I've got Don Chailey's photo…'
2 'I must do this; report the dead…'
3 'Either they saw us put the stuff on board and plan to track us to our destination.' 'Or?' 'They're…'
4 'Don't count your chickens,' she said eventually. 'I…'
5 'It is not fair…'
6 'Our own fears are our worst enemies…'
7 'First because we don't have a flag…'
8 'There'll be no lipstick or high-heels…'
9 'The American ambassador won't be pleased to learn that an American photographer…'
10 'Unless we fight back, all roads in future…'

Chapter 7

A colleague of Don Chailey's, Jack Normanton, arrives from America looking for him. Isa leaves a message for Jack Normanton at the international press agency to meet her at three p.m. in the Quinta Normale.

Andres is tortured with electric shocks. His body is in excruciating pain but his brain remains unaffected. He successfully resists giving any useful information until his torturers are thankfully interrupted by a young person who comes to tell them that the CNI is unable to verify Andres' story. The young voice also informs the Snake that Father Mariano has died as a result of their torture. At this news the Hog beats Andres unconscious.

Isa meets Jack Normanton and gives him the photographs. Beto has arranged for them to give a puppet show at the San Miguel market.

Andres is left for dead by the river, along with several other dead prisoners. He manages to crawl away from the pile of bodies. His body is discovered by Rosa, a farmer's daughter, who thinks Andres looks like her dead brother Tonio. The farmer is reluctant to help Andres out of fear, but eventually gives in to his daughter. He applies basic first aid to Andres and is honoured when he learns that Andres is Juan Larreta's son.

'This press conference, gentlemen, is now at an end.'

Repression

Colonel Rugeros, the spokesman for the Junta at the international gathering of journalists at the Ministry of Information, evades Jack Normanton's questions about the disappearance of Don Chailey. One way the Junta represses the intervention of other nations is by refusing to give out important information. It is almost impossible for visitors from other countries searching for missing relatives to get any co-operation from the Junta. Jack Normanton is no exception. How would the Junta view Normanton?

Narrative style and technique

Watson interweaves two stories in this chapter. He simultaneously tells the story of Andres' torture and the story of Jack Normanton and Isa. One reason he does this is to convey the feeling of events happening at the same time. In what other ways is this technique effective, particularly for the events of this chapter?

'And yet, unbelievably, his mind stayed where it was, unmolested, a little black box inside something nothing could get at.'

Andres

Andres experiences the biggest challenges of his life in this chapter. Firstly, his mental resilience is challenged during the torture session. Despite the horrific electric shocks he suffers, he never breaks down and confesses. Secondly, his physical strength is challenged as he fights for his life at the end of the chapter.

Andres' survival is facilitated by many instances of good luck. Firstly, he figures out that no one else has confessed. Secondly, his false story cannot be verified. Thirdly, Father Mariano also gives the name Horacio as the name of the Resistance soldier treated at the seminary. Without these three key events, what probably would have happened to him?

'Ring-leader of the Resistance.'

Diego Rosales, despite being badly crippled, is still a threat to the CNI. They

Diego Rosales

suspect that he is the ring-leader of the Resistance movement. Diego has obviously left his printshop and gone into hiding. Andres has to be very careful when Diego's name is mentioned as he cannot let on that he knows Diego. How does the Snake try to trap Andres with the mention of Diego's name? How does Andres get out of the trap?

'No man has ever died at my hands.'

The report of the death of Father Mariano to the interrogators marks the

Snake and Hog

turning point in Andres' torture session. Andres is astounded that the Snake is upset by the death of Father Mariano. What does the death of the priest mean to the Snake? The interrogators briefly switch roles in their reactions. How did you feel about the torturers after this scene? What prompts the Hog to beat Andres unconscious?

Think about how the Snake would react, following Andres' release. How would he treat the Hog? What would he report to his superiors? How would he feel about his job now that someone has 'died at his hands'? See the specimen coursework question on page 60.

'These pictures are a cause for celebration...'

Freedom/
resistance

The meeting between Isa and Jack Normanton is crucial to the resolution of the story. Jack will be able to get Don Chailey's photographs on the front page of newspapers around the world. Once the truth is known, foreign governments will intervene and monitor the activities of the Junta. Most importantly, these governments will fight against human rights violations.

How does juxtaposing of Andres' torture next to Isa's meeting with Jack Normanton effectively bring out the conflict between the two political ideologies? For more information see question 2 of the example exam questions on page 57.

'Dumped, rib broken; maybe more than one. Eyes swollen, flesh to the bone; blood in trickles from his hair, his nose. Groin afire with pain.'

The description of Andres' torture and after effects are the most brutal scenes in the novel. What effect did these scenes have on you? Although some readers might find these scenes disturbing, why is it vital that they are included?

Read this section again. There are many incomplete sentences. What is the effect of the way this is written?

Brutality

'And love's not something that gets smaller if you divide it up. I'll never believe that!'

Isa and Beto come close to arguing in this chapter. It is only natural that siblings argue and, moreover, that Beto would be jealous of Andres. Luckily Isa's diplomatic skills enable her to reassure Beto about Andres and strike a compromise about performing at the orphanage.

Triumph of the human spirit

'The farmer was torn between compassion and fear.'

The farmer saves Andres' life by applying basic first aid and giving him food and drink. Why is Francisco reluctant at first to help Andres? Why does he change his mind?

The turning point of the novel is reached in this chapter. In fact the narrative has been split into two stories since Chapter 4, so that there are in effect two turning points. Identify these turning points and keep track of how the story is resolved from this point on.

Chapter Eight

It is Sunday, a week since the assassination of the Miguel Alberti. Thousands of people have been arrested and hundreds killed in the Junta's search for friends and supporters of the Silver Lion. Santiago is under military occupation until the leaders of the Resistance movement are arrested. All roads into Santiago have road blocks and every vehicle is being checked.

Francisco's van is stopped by Security on the way through the suburbs of Santiago. Andres, in the back of the van, suppresses a cough and Rosa distracts the soldier by pointing out a lorry transporting sharks. After making it through the inspection, Andres thinks he is dying.

At the San Miguel market a crowd stares at Andres and warns Francisco that the market is crawling with Black Berets. Andres, drunk on wine, announces that he is Juan Larreta's son and the crowd offer their support to his courage.

When Rosa mentions a puppet show, Andres knows that Isa and Beto must be there. Rosa walks him over to the twins' van and helps him into the back. Meanwhile, Isa makes the crowd laugh by mocking General Zuckerman with her new puppet, General Zuckero. The people of Chile are fighting back by asking General Zuckero the truth about missing relatives, reports of executions and the murder of the Silver Lion. The laughter of the crowd draws the attention of the Black Berets, but the crowd help the twins make a safe getaway.

On their way out of Santiago, the twins' van is inspected but the Black Berets fail to notice Andres. The twins believe Andres is dead and stop for lunch where they shared their first meal with him. Beto discovers Andres in the back of the van and the three friends are reunited.

'Andres was quivering with life.'

Triumph of the human spirit

Andres is convinced he is dying. When, however, he hears the mention of the puppet show at the market, his spirit is rejuvenated. He is hopeful and joyful at the thought of seeing Isa again. Despite his physical suffering, the power of love gives him the will to live. Do you think Andres would have survived if he hadn't been reunited with his friends? What is Watson saying about the relationship between the body and the spirit?

'Proud as a peacock, the General strutted into the sunlight, medals gleaming, moustache fluffed and groomed, helmet polished and plumed.'

General Zuckerman

The above quote actually describes the entrance of the puppet General Zuckero. Isa uses this puppet to mock the real General. What to do you expect General Zuckerman to be like based on the puppet's appearance and attitude?

Narrative style and technique

The introduction of the puppet General Zuckero into the show marks the beginning of the climax of the novel. A great deal of tension is created in this scene. Firstly, Rosa is delivering Andres to the twins' van at the same time that Isa retrieves General Zuckero from their van. Thus, Isa and Andres narrowly miss each other. Isa would not be looking for Andres, so it is understandable that she did not see him. Andres, on the other hand, knows that Isa is there but cannot look out for her because he is half blind.

Secondly, Isa and Beto have conflicting feelings about using the puppet. Beto is anxious that they could get arrested. In fact, he argued with Isa about even bringing the contentious puppet to the market. Why is the puppet dangerous? Isa feels that it is important that they resist the Junta in any way they can. Fear will only lead them to conform to the Junta's expectations.

Thirdly, although the crowd laughs at the mocking of General Zuckerman, Beto is afraid that there might be a spy among them, or that the laughter might attract the attention of the Black Berets who patrol the market. Tension is created through the contrast of laughter and danger. Notice too that the nature of the laughter itself changes once Zuckero enters the show. The crowd laugh at the visual humour of the skeleton knocking a man under the chin and Orlando the Ostrich pecking a lady's nose. When the crowd laugh at General Zuckero, however, they are really laughing with Isa in her satirising of General Zuckerman's betrayal of the people of Chile. How do the two types of humour differ?

Finally, when the twins flee the market they do not know that Andres is in the back of their van. This creates suspense because we wonder how Andres' presence will be revealed to them.

How does the collective behaviour of those who resist help highlight the conflict between the two political ideologies when compared to the behaviour of those in power? For more information see question 2 of the examle exam questions on page 57.

'Well for once we've nothing to hide.'

Watson also uses irony to create tension and suspense. When the twins are stopped by Security the tension is heightened because they are ignorant of the true danger they are in by concealing Andres.

Narrative style and technique

'Isa was remembering their mother and father – disappeared.'

Beto stops Isa from getting carried away in her mocking of General Zuckerman. She is a sensible girl and thinks immediately about all the people that she loves who have disappeared. Although it is gratifying for her to discover the crowd is behind her in her criticism of General Zuckerman, it is more important to her that she remains on the good side of the Junta. Why is it vital that she doesn't get arrested?

Isa

'I'm back, friends… Need restringing.'

Andres cracks this joke when Rosa helps him into the back of the twins' van with the other puppets. Andres has been described as a puppet since the

Andres

beginning of the torture scene in Chapter 7. The imagery is two-fold. Firstly, Andres is like a puppet to the torturers who controlled his movement with the electric shocks, with the wires acting as the puppeteer's strings. Secondly, Andres is denied all human rights by the Snake and the Hog. They could do as they pleased with him, so he is treated not as a human being but as the Junta's puppet. Thirdly, as a result of his injuries, Andres' movement resembles the fragmented movement of puppets.

'I think I made it, Isa!'

The twins and Andres are fully reconciled, both physically and emotionally

Triumph of the human spirit

at the end of this chapter. Beto accepts that Isa has fallen in love with Andres and that he has more to lose by being jealous of Andres than welcoming him into his life. Andres manages to survive excruciating pain and horrific injuries in order to see Isa again. Isa and Beto narrowly escape being arrested, and having Andres unwittingly arrested. How has Watson made this closing scene dramatic? Now that the friends are together again, what do you predict will follow?

The crowd play an important part in this chapter in helping Isa and Beto escape. Examiners will expect you to know the contribution that minor characters have made to the development of theme, development of character and establishing of setting. Consider the significance of all the minor characters.

Epilogue

The Two Hemispheres Trophy competition is taking place at the stadium of Santiago between England and Chile. There are no traces of the atrocities which recently took place there. General Zuckerman sits in the Box of State. Earlier in the day he had assured the Archbishop of Santiago that Security knew nothing of Father Mariano, who allegedly died as a result of torture. Soon after the match commences, the Director of the State Information Services shows General Zuckerman that morning's front page of the Baltimore Express & Times featuring the leading story on the assassination of Miguel Alberti, written by the recently expelled journalist, Jack Normanton. General Zuckerman and his ministers leave the box to discuss the matter.

At half time, Isa and Beto are among many people distributing leaflets carrying Don Chailey's photograph and eye witness account of the assassination of the Silver Lion. These leaflets are being distributed all over Chile. It is the beginning for those who resist, such as Andres. He watches Isa whom he loves, and sees soldiers destroying the leaflets. He has tears in his eyes of hope and despair.

**Narrative style
and technique**

An epilogue is a short speech at the end of a literary work.
Why is this last section an epilogue and not another chapter?

'In the stadium of Santiago a massive crowd awaits the arrival of the teams in the opening match of the Two Hemispheres Trophy competition.'

The story begins and ends in the stadium of Santiago. One effect of this is to provide closure to the story. It ends where it began, but we have moved from Miguel Alberti's presence there as the almost elected leader, to General Cesar Zuckerman's as the leader by force. What is ironic about this setting? Whose voice narrates the entire Epilogue?

'It seems that none of it actually happened, just as the atrocities committed after the assassination of President Allende in 1973 did not happen.'

Brutality

President Salvador Allende's government was overthrow in a coup d'état in 1973. Allende died in combat, and many of his supporters were arrested, tortured and killed by General Pinochet's army. Then, as now, those arrested were initially brought to the stadium. Pinochet's security force denied all allegations of human rights violations. They even claimed that Allende committed suicide, despite widespread belief that he was assassinated.

Zuckerman's army, like Pinochet's before him, has cleaned up the stadium and erased any evidence of what suffering and death really went on.

'It is not acceptable to me, Archbishop, to be told that your priests take it upon themselves to be critics of the government.'

General Zuckerman denies all knowledge of Father Mariano to the Archbishop of Santiago, and denies claims that the priest died as a result of torture. We know that this is a lie. To exert his power and discourage the Archbishop of Santiago from pursuing the cause of Father Mariano's death, General Zuckerman rebukes the Archbishop as representative of his priests who criticise the government. What does this scene add to your knowledge of the general?

'But for those who resist, there will be a beginning.'

The beginning comes in the form of the morning edition of the *Baltimore Express & Times* featuring Jack Normanton's cover story. This story will

**Freedom/
resistance**

certainly get the attention of the rest of the world. The involvement of other governments is the Resistance movement's best chance of ridding their country of General Zuckerman's regime.

The distribution of the leaflets up and down Chile marks the end of people having to whisper. How is the equalising of the score by the Chilean team symbolic of the people of Chile?

'There are tears in Andres' eyes, for his lost father; but they are not tears only of despair.'

Andres

In Chapter 2 we were told that Andres had planned to go to this game with Juan, Horacio and Braulio. Although he has found love with Isa, being at the game reminds him of his lost father and friends. He must wonder whether Juan and Braulio are still alive.

Andres' face has changed as a result of the torture he suffered. Consider the multiple meanings of Watson's description that Andres' face is '... the face of his age'.

Watson said in an interview that the book ends on an 'up note'. The other tears in Andres' eyes are tears of hope. Explore the elements of hope in this epilogue.

The story ends where it began, at the National stadium, hence achieving the structural effects of balance and closure. Examiners will expect you to be aware of all structural devices used in the novel. What other events are balanced or paralleled? Now that you have read the novel through once, pay close attention to other structural devices as you reread the novel several times for revision.

■ Self-test Questions Chapters 7, 8 and the Epilogue

Uncover the plot

Delete two of the three alternatives given to find the correct plot. Beware possible misconceptions and muddles.

A colleague/friend/relative of Don Chailey's arrives in Chile to look for him. His name is Francisco Herrera/Jack Normanton/Hernando Salas and he is a journalist for the *Baltimore Times/Mercury/Philadelphia Star*. Francisco Herrera/Jack Normanton/Hernando Salas attends the international gathering of armies/

journalists/photographers at the Ministry of Information in San Jose/San Miguel/Santiago. He tries to get answers from Miguel Alberti/Colonel Rugeros/General Zuckerman about Don Chailey, but the spokesman for the Communists/Democrats/Junta evades all questions. When he returns to the offices of the international press agency, there is a telephone message from Andres/Isa/Rosa. The message asks him to meet her at the quarry/Quinta Normale/seminary and to look out for her green panama/puppets/van.

Andres' body is badly hurt during the electric shock/heat/water torture, but his mind stays alert. His torture session is interrupted by the news that his story cannot be finished/true/verified and that Don Chailey/Father Mariano/Juan Larreta is dead. Andres is beaten unconscious and his body is dumped along the quarry/river/seaside.

Isa meets up with Francisco Herrera/Jack Normanton/Hernando Salas at the mill/park/seminary and gives him Don Chailey's camera/photographs/wallet. He says that the photographs/recordings/stories will make the front page on newspapers around America/Chile/the world.

Beto has arranged for himself and Andres/Diego/Isa to perform at the San Jose hospital/orphanage/stadium. Isa is anxious/pleased/reluctant to leave Santiago when Andres/Jack/Juan is missing. Beto fears that Andres/Jack/Juan is coming between them, but Isa reassures him that she can love both/neither/one of them.

Andres manages to move himself away from the other dead bodies along the quarry/river/seaside. He is saved by a farmer/journalist/minister and his daughter/son/wife.

A week after the assassination of Miguel Alberti/Don Chailey/Juan Larreta, Santiago is under military occupation and all aeroplanes/people/vehicles coming in and out of the city are inspected. Andres makes it safely to the market/mill/quarry in the back of Beto's/Francisco's/Tonio's van. He thinks he is dying/ill/scared, but is inspired when he learns that his father/friends/torturers are performing at the market/orphanage/park. Francisco/Rosa/Tonio helps him hide in the back of the twin's van. Isa and Beto avoid arrest once/twice/three times and are reunited with Andres when they stop for breakfast/lunch/dinner at the mill/park/quarry.

A short time later, the orphanage/stadium/station of Santiago is cleaned up and the Two Cities/Hemispheres/Nations Trophy is played between Chile and America/England/Italy. There are many/no/some traces of the suffering and death which took place here. General Zuckerman/Juan/Snake watches the game from the State Box. Earlier in the day he had commended/reprimanded/thanked the Archbishop of San Jose/San Miguel/Santiago for suggesting that the Security was involved in the death of Miguel Alberti/Father Mariano/Sister Theresa. The Director of State Information Services disturbs General Zuckerman to show him the front page of the *Baltimore Express & Times/Mercury/Philadelphia Star* which carries a story by Don Chailey/Andres Larreta/Jack Normanton and a huge picture of Miguel Alberti/Salvador Allende/Horacio Rivera at the moment of his assassination. All over the orphanage/stadium/station of Santiago leaflets are also being distributed featuring Don Chailey's/Jack Normanton's/Diego Rosales' photographs and testimony of the assassination of the Hog/Silver Lion/Snake. These same leaflets are being distributed all over America/Chile/Peru. Andres fancies/likes/loves Isa and watches her circulate the leaflets/newspapers/tickets in the stands. He thinks of his father/friends/mother. There are tears in his eyes, but they are of hope as well as despair/self pity/terror.

Who? What? Why? When? Where? How?

1   Who are distributing the leaflets at the football match?
2   How did the secretary know that Isa was genuine when she rang for Jack Normanton?

3 Of whom does Andres remind Francisco and Rosa ?
4 What do the Hog and the Snake think Andres was doing when he was caught?
5 Who asks General Zuckerman about Father Mariano?
6 How does the crowd help the twins get away safely from the market?
7 Why had Don Chailey gone to Chile?
8 What match is played in the stadium?
9 Where do the twins stop for lunch?
10 When does the reporter at the press conference say that Don Chailey went missing?

Who says that, and to whom?
1 'Do not take my word for it... simply look!'
2 'He died in my care.'
3 'Shut it! Unless you really want us stuck up against a wall.'
4 'We can't get involved.'
5 'Church and State must be as one against the common enemy.'
6 'Our Tonio was nice like you.'
7 'They'll be on every front page from Alaska to Australia.'
8 'Anybody... anybody at home?'
9 'I alone have rescued Chile from a fate worse than death.'
10 'This press conference, gentlemen, is now at an end.'

Open quotes
Identify the scene; complete the phrase; identify the speaker and the character being spoken to.
1 'Tonio had no one to help him...'
2 'I'm not going to answer a stranger's questions unless I'm given the secret password.' 'I'm...'
3 'Any passengers in the back?' 'Not...'
4 'You, Sis have gone crazy!... But...'
5 'Order in Chile has been restored:...'
6 'They could have shot me for cheek.' 'True...'
7 'You think Andres has come between us –...'
8 'Is it sleep –...'
9 'For old time's sake...'
10 'Did Mariano make his confession?' 'To his...'

How to write an examination essay

Talking in Whispers is a popular text for diverse culture and tradition work in English, but it is also an English literature examination text with at least one examination board. Preparing for an examination essay is different from preparing for a coursework assignment.

General advice about the types of literature examination questions

There are two popular types of literature examination question. One type of question asks you to write about the presentation of a specific theme or character throughout the text. The second type of question asks you to focus on a specific passage or section from the text. Each type of question addresses a central conflict in the text and you must show your understanding of the issues presented in the novel surrounding this conflict. For instance, to answer the sample question, *Show how James Watson brings out the conflict between democracy on the one hand, and rule by force on the other*, you are really being asked to demonstrate your understanding of these two political systems and the variety of ways in which Watson presents them, such as through contrasting settings, atmospheres, characters and narrative styles. More detail on how to answer this question appears on page 57.

If the question is of the second type, which asks you to focus on a certain chapter or passage of the novel, make sure that you refer to the entire text. Always demonstrate that you know how the conflict presented in the passage is initially introduced and eventually resolved. For instance, if you are asked to focus on Andres' torture in Chapter 6, you must remember to mention how Watson prepared us for this by describing the increasing brutality of the Junta as seen in the beating of Braulio in Chapter 2 and the physical appearance of Diego Rosales, a former torture victim, in Chapter 3. You must also mention how Andres comes to be released in Chapter 7 and the consequences of his beatings, such as his physical injuries.

How to approach the question

Make sure that you understand precisely what the question is asking you to do. It is a good idea to underline the key words in the question. The key words in the above sample question are *how Watson brings out the conflict between democracy and rule by force.*

After you have identified the exact nature of the task demanded by the question, spend five to ten minutes planning your answer. Examiners comment every year that the more successful candidates are those who carefully plan their answers. In planning your answer, identify and make brief notes on the key points from the novel that are appropriate to answering the question. A good rule of thumb is to have at least three key points to discuss. Jot down key quotations from the novel that emphasise the significance of the key points. Order these key events to give your essay a sense of structure. Finally in your plan, have an idea of where your argument is leading and how you will conclude your essay. For example, if you were answering the sample question above, you could conclude your essay by giving your personal reaction to the presentation of the political conflict. An alternative conclusion could be to discuss how Watson ends the novel on a hopeful note in favour of democracy. Do not spend more than ten minutes planning your answer.

Putting pen to paper

Your opening sentences are important. Try to summarise your response to the question so the examiner has some idea of how you are going to approach it. Do not say 'I am going to write about the conflict between democracy and rule by force presented in the novel', but instead write 'The assassination of The Silver Lion at the start of *Talking in Whispers* marks the beginning of the conflict between democracy and rule by force explored throughout the novel'. Make sure that you define any necessary concepts such as *democracy* and *rule by force*. After the introductory paragraph plunge straight into discussing your key points. DO NOT RETELL THE STORY. Make sure that you include textual references to back up your main points. As you write your essay *constantly refer back to your list of key points* and make sure that you are actually responding to them. Examiners reward candidates who can highlight alternative interpretations of meaning and make comparisons within the text. Do include your personal interpretation, as examiners reward your ideas as long as you can back them up with evidence from the text.

A word about quotation

Do not quote reams of text. Long textual references are no substitute for a lack of argument or ideas. The most successful quotations are imbedded within the point a candidate is trying to make. As general rule never quote more than a sentence.

How long should it be?

There is no 'correct' length. It is your timing that is most important. Allocate the time spent on each question according to the percentage of marks awarded to it. For instance, if you need to answer two questions earning equal marks in two hours, you should spend an hour on each question. In answering each question you should spend up to ten minutes planning your answer and five minutes checking it over at the end.

Technical points to keep in mind

- Write your essay in formal English. Never use slang and do not write as if you were speaking.
- Avoid using contractions. Write '*should have*' not '*should've*'.
- Organise your essay into paragraphs.
- Check your spelling. Accurate spelling is rewarded. Careless spelling mistakes create a bad impression.
- Use punctuation appropriately and correctly. Do not confuse the possessive apostrophe with plurals.
- Take care over the presentation of your essay. Write legibly and avoid crossing out too many words or sentences. Many crossings out indicate a lack of planning.

Example questions

Below are two examples of the kinds of questions you may expect in your exam. An *outline* of a model answer has been supplied. You will find it useful to write full-length versions of these plans, incorporating references from the text to back up the ideas.

1   There are many times in the text when Andres is in danger. Choose two or three such incidents and answer both parts of the question.

   (a) Explain the dangers which face Andres in each of your chosen episodes.

   (b) Write about the ways in which the writer builds up a sense of suspense, fear and excitement in these episodes.

NEAB specimen 1998

Include the following points for (a):

- Choose three obvious examples of danger, such as when Juan's car is forced off the road, the torture scenes and Don Chailey's meeting with Andres.
- Discriminate between physical, psychological and political danger.
- Explore the social/cultural/historical contexts.
- Use appropriate close textual references and precise detail.

Include the following points for (b):

- Define and differentiate between suspense, fear and excitement. Suspense is a state of uncertainty while awaiting news or an event. Fear is distress or alarm caused by impending danger or pain. Excitement is the state of heightened emotion.
- Analyse Watson's technique such as the structure of the chosen passages, vocabulary, syntax (word order), speech, description and point of view.

- Use structural analysis to explain the build up of suspense, fear or excitement.
- Use appropriate close textual references and precise detail.

- Divide your time equally between the two parts of the question.
- Explaining the dangers which face Andres means discussing your chosen episodes in terms of cause and effect. Make sure that you avoid the trap of merely describing the dangers or narrating your chosen episodes.
- You should concentrate on narrative technique, style and structure in answering the second half of the question.

2 Show how James Watson brings out the conflict between democracy on the one hand, and rule by the force of arms on the other.

Include the following points:

NEAB specimen 1998

- Democracy is associated with the characters of the Silver Lion, Juan Larreta, Andres, Isa, Beto, Don Chailey, Jack Normanton and Diego Rosales.
- Rule by force is associated with General Zuckerman, the CNI and the Junta.

The contrast between these two political states is highlighted through:

- The individual behaviour and revelation of characters, such as the loyalty and camaraderie of Andres and the twins versus the petty squabbles of the Snake and the Hog.
- The collective behaviour of those who resist versus the collective behaviour of those in power.
- The juxtaposing of events, such as Andres' torture next to Isa's meeting with Jack Normanton.
- An analysis of the ideologies in their social/cultural/historical context.

You should also show an awareness of Watson's aims in writing this book, and use of appropriate close textual references and precise detail.

- Refer to the entire novel.
- Define the concepts of 'democracy' and 'rule by force'.
- Discuss how Watson brings out this conflict in three different ways; through contrasting characters, through narrative structure and through contrasting themes.

How to write a coursework essay

Many of you may use *Talking in Whispers* for coursework reflecting diverse cultures and traditions. The main assessment criterion for 'diverse cultures and traditions' coursework is to present your understanding of the culture presented in the text you have studied. It is important that you make notes about the Chilean culture presented as you read *Talking in Whispers*. One reason that we read novels set in different cultures is to widen our knowledge of the diversity of cultures around the world. Many cultures have social and literary traditions which are different from our own. Knowledge and experience of this diversity help us to widen our perceptions, and open our minds to alternative ways of viewing the world.

Talking in Whispers does not present a diverse cultural tradition because the author, James Watson, is an English author writing for an English audience. It does, however, present a culture that is different from English culture. In fact, one of Watson's aims in writing this novel was to present the difficulties faced by teenagers living in an undemocratic society, where they are denied basic human rights. In preparation for your coursework make notes on the following cultural features:

- settings – landscape, climate, season, time period;
- importance of family relationships and friendships;
- the political system;
- the society presented – are there economic or gender inequalities within society?
- the importance of religion;
- details on diet, fashion, standard of living, entertainment, etc;
- the values and beliefs presented.

As well as demonstrating your awareness of the cultural issues presented in the novel, your coursework task will also require you to demonstrate your knowledge and understanding of a character, a relationship, a theme, genre or literary device, such as imagery, presented in the novel. The nature of the actual coursework can be discursive, creative or empathetic.

- A *discursive* essay requires you to discuss an aspect of the novel in a formal, argumentative essay. These essays are the most common type of examination essay set. Sometimes a discursive essay will require you to criticise the novel from a literary point of view. An example of a literary criticism assignment would be to discuss the success of *Talking in Whispers* as a political thriller. Discursive essays require lots of textual references to back up your ideas. Much of the advice in the section on **How to write an examination essay** applies to discursive coursework essays too.

- A *creative* response requires you to write about the novel in an imaginative way. An example of a creative response assignment would be to write the next chapter of the novel. When writing creative responses to literature you must try to write in the style of the author, maintain features of the text such as settings and imagery, develop aspects of the text (such as characters and theme) in a plausible way, and sustain the story in an imaginative and interesting way. Many students prefer writing creative responses to discursive essays because creative responses build on story writing skills. Make sure that you include cultural features such as the importance of comradeship in your response.

- An *empathetic* response to the novel requires you to write from the point of view of one of the characters. This type of essay demonstrates your knowledge of that character and their point of view, which may be different from the author's point of view or the point of view of the narrator. An example of an empathetic response essay would be to write Isa's diary.

- It is not always desirable to use direct textual references in creative or empathetic response essays. You are, however, still expected to make reference to the text. In each type of essay it is often more appropriate to demonstrate your knowledge of the text by imbedding references to incidents in your narrative rather than by using direct textual quotation. The textual commentary notes denoted by the narrative style icon in this book will be especially helpful for any type of coursework.

Writing the coursework essay

- It is essential that you make a plan before you begin to write. Think about the key points of the novel that are relevant to your essay. You will also need to decide what stylistic features you will include in your essay. For instance, a stylistic feature of discursive essays is to write in formal, Standard English. Empathetic response essays, on the other hand, usually require you to write in the 'role' of a character who may have a distinctive accent or dialect. It is appropriate in these essays to imitate the rhythms and grammar of the speech used by the characters.

- Always do a rough draft of your coursework. Listen to the suggestions that your teacher makes after reading your rough draft and amend your draft accordingly.

- Check your best draft carefully for spelling, punctuation and grammar.

How long should my essay be?

Most coursework should be a minimum of 500 words, and as long as it needs to be to answer the question fully and well. Remember that a long essay is not necessarily a good one; make sure that everything you write is concise and relevant. Check with your teacher for specific word limits. Also check with your teacher if you are allowed to word process your essay.

Example question

Below is an example of the kind of question you may expect for your coursework assignment. An *outline* of a model answer has been supplied for the question. You will find it useful to write a full-length version of this plan, incorporating references from the text to back up the ideas.

Write an imaginative response to the text in the form of Snake's Diary.

In this essay you should include the following points:

- The Junta's capture of Juan Larreta. The Snake would not like Juan Larreta because Juan sings anti-government songs. He would be looking forward to torturing Juan. Juan's songs attack the rich and generals in the army for tyranny (Chapter 2).

- The murder of The Silver Lion. The Snake would rejoice in Alberti's death (Chapter 1). The Snake would know who murdered Alberti.

- References to General Zuckerman, leader of the Republic and the armed forces, because he is the Snake's boss.

- References to the House of Laughter where the Snake works, described in Chapter 2.

- The CNI soldiers are after Hernando Salas when they capture Andres. He may be the wounded Resistance fighter who is brought into the Seminary the night that Andres is captured.

- Entries for the torture of Andres in Chapters 6 and 7. Andres is released in Chapter 7.

- The Snake would express his sadness and disappointment at the news of Father Mariano's death in Chapter 7.

- For comic effect, mention the Snake's feelings about the Hog.

- Be exact about the dates of the entries. The Silver Lion was assassinated on a Saturday. This is the same day that Juan is arrested. Andres is arrested in the early hours of the following Saturday and tortured later that day.

- REMEMBER: You are trying to convey the feelings of a torturer and supporter of the Junta.

- Use an appropriate 'voice' for the Snake. Go back and reread Chapters 6 and 7. Pay attention to how Watson presents the Snake and try to write in the same spirit. Do, however, also write in a style appropriate to a personal diary.

- You can use direct textual references if you are careful about incorporating them into your diary entry. Alternatively, you can fulfil the requirement for textual references by referring to suitable key events in your diary entries.

Self-test Answers Chapters 1–3

Uncover the plot

The story opens the day before the presidential elections in Chile. Twenty thousand people have come to the stadium of Santiago to hear the election speech of Miguel Alberti, affectionately known as the Silver Lion. The popular trio Los Obstinados play at the proceedings. On their way to San Jose the trio's car is shot at by the Black Berets. Horacio is killed. Andres Larreta is thrown clear but watches his father, Juan, being beaten by the soldiers. Andres gets a lift to San Jose in a van with the twins Isa and Beto. The twins are puppeteers. At a road block they learn that Miguel Alberti has been shot while making his final election speech in San Jose. The Junta takes control of the situation and imposes a curfew. The Junta blames the assassination on the Communists. Beto, Isa and Andres return to Santiago. On the outskirts of Santiago they hear gunfire. They abandon the van while the tanks and soldiers pass.

The next day the National Stadium has been turned into an interrogation centre. Andres has a nightmare about the death of his mother. *The Mercury* newspaper reports that Juan and Andres were killed in the car accident. The Security know that Andres is still alive. The next day Andres visits the homes of the friends and families of Los Obstinados. On his way he sees a youth shot dead by the Black Berets. He also learns that the homes of Juan's friends have been visited by the CNI and the men have been arrested. Andres returns to the stadium and sees Braulio. Andres meets an American journalist who gives his camera to Andres when he is spotted taking photographs by the Black Berets.

Against the advice of Isa, Andres returns to his house. The Black Berets ransack the house and burn Juan's possessions. An officer declares Juan an enemy of the state. An Indian man who protests is bundled into an army van. Andres returns to the mill and tells Isa and Beto about the camera. He manages to save a leaflet from Juan's house. On the leaflet is the address of Horacio's cousin, Diego, who owns a printshop. The three visit Diego after curfew. Although his shop has been ransacked, the CNI found nothing, as they missed his darkroom. Diego develops the photos. They contain evidence that the Junta assassinated Miguel Alberti. The three are keen to help the Resistance movement, but Diego warns them that it is very dangerous.

Who? What? Why? When? Where? How?

1   San Jose.
2   Miguel Alberti (the Silver Lion).
3   An Inca princess.
4   Andres' 'posh' cord bomber jacket distinguished him as someone from Santiago and not the surrounding countryside.
5   Highland Helen because her father was from Scotland.
6   It was disguised as a Ladies' room.
7   To make it more difficult for people to get together to form a Resistance movement against the Junta.
8   Andres remembers that the Araucanos Indians resisted the Spanish conquerors for three hundred and fifty years. He draws a parallel between what the Spanish conquerors did to the Indians and his own situation.
9   To cover up the fact that they murdered Alberti themselves.
10 At a school for under school-age children of working families.

Who says that, and to whom?

1 An officer after arresting the Indian man for defending Juan Larreta's good name. Chapter 3.
2 Beto describing Isa's dominance to Andres. Chapter 1.
3 Beto to Isa about Andres after discovering his true identify from the story of his supposed death in the newspaper. Chapter 2.
4 Andres lying to Isa and Beto about why he is hitching a ride. Chapter 1.
5 Isa to Andres about the danger involved in visiting Diego's printshop. Chapter 3.
6 Andres to the Black Berets after they shoot the youth with the long hair. Chapter 2.
7 Isa describing Andres to Diego. Chapter 3.
8 General Zuckerman to the people of Chile during his broadcast following the assassination of the Silver Lion. He is trying to throw suspicion off his own regime. Chapter 1.
9 Diego Rosales describing the friends with whom he has distributed the parts of his printing press. Chapter 3.
10 Don Chailey handing his camera to Andres before he is taken prisoner by the Black Berets. Chapter 2.

Open quotes

1 '… send the soldiers back to their barracks – where they belong!' Miguel Alberti to the people of Chile the day before the elections. Chapter 1.
2 'For just seeing these pictures they'd kill us.' Isa remarking on how dangerous it would be if the Junta found out about Don Chailey's photographs. Chapter 3.
3 'Of course the Security too were at the graveside: they took the names of all the mourners.' Andres recalling the CNI's presence at his mother's funeral. Chapter 2.
4 'You want to help? Okay, but understand this – there's no going back.' Diego Rosales about the commitment needed once one joins the Resistance movement. Chapter 3.
5 '… am I really doing this for Dad, for glory or just to show off in front of this dream of a girl…?', Andres contemplates his real motives for risking his life to see what is going on. Chapter 1.
6 'He must have been crazy, taking such risks. And for what? For glory?' 'For the truth, maybe,' Isa's response to the question of why the American risked his life to take the photographs. Chapter 3.
7 'We checked your brain – it's still intact.' Beto making light of Andres' near escape from a bullet the night before. Chapter 2.
8 'Brothers take running jumps at things – and then think about the distance when it's too late.' Isa describing Beto to Andres. Chapter 1.
9 '… people were relieved – sometimes eager – to see him leave.' Andres notices that the women at the homes of his friends are afraid to talk to him and to be seen with him. Chapter 2.
10 'All you'll be needing is a cool head, lots of luck – and… And a porter's uniform.' Diego Rosales describing his plan to Isa, Beto and Andres. Chapter 3.

Self-test Answers Chapters 4–6

Uncover the plot

There are six thousand prisoners at the stadium and more are brought every hour. Andres and the twins carry out Diego's plan on Friday at the Santiago train station. Andres is dressed up as a porter. Diego's friends leave parts of the printing press in the lockers and drop the keys into Isa's panama. Andres retrieves the keys, collects the items from the lockers and wheels them on a trolley to the van. Andres and the twins successfully collect all the parts of the printing press and drive away. They are followed, so they head out of town. Andres is dropped off with the sacks and he hides them in a quarry. The twins lose their followers at a school. Andres sees prisoners shot at the quarry. He checks the bodies to see if Juan is among them. Don Chailey is among the dead. Andres finds the journalist's press card. Andres will try to contact the families of the men he could identify.

There is a five-hour gun battle between the Junta and the Resistance. The ring-leaders of the Resistance escape. Isa worries that the escaped ring-leaders will go to Father Mariano's seminary to hide. Andres goes to the seminary for the night because he does not have time to get back to the mill before curfew. Against the orders of the Archbishop, Father Mariano lets Andres stay. During the night, a wounded Resistance soldier is brought in followed by a doctor. Later the Security arrive and beat up Father Mariano. Andres escapes from the seminary, only to be captured by the Black Berets.

Isa has a nightmare about Andres. She tries to visit the seminary straight away, but Beto makes her see sense about the danger of going out during the curfew hours. Andres is taken to the House of Laughter. A hood is put over his head so that he cannot identify his interrogators. He nicknames his interrogators Hog and Snake. He is badly beaten and his nose is broken. He does not give his interrogators any useful information so they prepare to torture him with electric shock treatment. Later in the day, Isa visits the seminary. Sister Theresa has a broken arm and bad bruising. Father Mariano has been taken away for questioning and Sister Theresa fears he will die if tortured because of his heart condition. She tells Isa that Andres was there the night before but not in the morning. She hopes that he escaped. She gives Isa a package that Andres had left. She relates Andres' story about the shooting of Don Chailey. Isa knows that this is valuable information.

Who? What? Why? When? Where? How?

1 Hugo Benedetti.
2 The ring-leader of the Resistance movement.
3 Friday.
4 In a quarry.
5 By beating, stretching and electric shock.
6 They think that they are protecting Hernando Salas.
7 Don Chailey.
8 The CNI shooting prisoners.
9 As soon as she woke up at quarter past five in the morning, before the end of the curfew.
10 She knew that he would not have been able to stay so calm if he had known.

Who says that, and to whom?

1 Beto trying to talk Isa out of visiting the seminary before the end of the curfew. Chapter 6.

2   Isa to Beto, fearing that she has put Andres into danger by suggesting that he spend the night at Father Mariano's seminary. Chapter 5.
3   The elderly lady to Andres when he loses his balance while lifting a suitcase and falls into her newspaper. Chapter 4.
4   Andres to Isa and Beto after narrowly escaping the Junta and the station supervisor while carrying out Diego's plan. Chapter 4.
5   Andres remembering Juan's advice about being interrogated. Chapter 6.
6   Father Mariano to Andres. Chapter 5.
7   The Black Berets to Andres as he tries to escape from the seminary. Chapter 5.
8   Isa to Beto when they avoid being arrested by the Security by driving past a school just as the children are let out. Chapter 4.
9   The Snake denying Andres his constitutional rights. Chapter 6.
10   Sister Theresa showing Isa where she has hidden Andres' package. Chapter 6.

Open quotes
1   'Under the front seat of the van, I've got Don Chailey's photos ... And I'm going to make all these things talk!' Isa to Sister Theresa. Chapter 6.
2   'I must do this; report the dead. For no one else on earth will.' Andres making up his mind to contact the families of the dead men at the quarry. Chapter 5.
3   'Either they saw us put the stuff on board and plan to track us to our destination' 'Or?' 'They're following us because they've nothing better to do.' Isa to Andres and Beto about why they are being followed. Chapter 4.
4   'Don't count your chickens,' she said eventually. 'I think we're being tailed.' Isa to Beto when they drive away from the station with the printing press. Chapter 4.
5   'It's not fair: and I must not cry.' Andres to himself when he is about to be tortured. Chapter 6.
6   'Our own fears are our worst enemies, not the reds ... ' The words written by Don Chailey that Andres finds on his dead body at the quarry. Chapter 5.
7   'First because we don't have a flag. Second, because we don't have a window.' Isa rejecting Beto's suggestion that they fly a national flag to throw the Security off their trail. Chapter 5.
8   'There'll be no lipstick or high-heels where they're being taken.' The soldier about the two girls who are arrested at the train station. Chapter 4.
9   'The American ambassador won't be pleased to learn that an American photographer was executed without trial by servants of the Junta.' Sister Theresa to Isa about Don Chailey's murder. Chapter 6.
10   'Unless we fight back, all roads in future will lead to the House of Laughter.' Andres is inspired by Diego's words. Chapter 5.

■ Self-test Answers Chapters 7, 8 and the Epilogue

Uncover the plot
A colleague of Don Chailey's arrives in Chile to look for him. His name is Jack Normanton and he is a journalist for the *Philadelphia Star*. Jack Normanton attends the international gathering of journalists at the Ministry of Information

in Santiago. He tries to get answers from Colonel Rugeros about Don Chailey, but the spokesman for the Junta evades all questions. When he returns to the offices of the international press agency, there is a telephone message from Isa. The message asks him to meet her at the Quinta Normale and to look out for her green panama.

Andres' body is badly hurt during the electric shock torture, but his mind stays alert. His torture session is interrupted by the news that his story cannot be verified and that Father Mariano is dead. Andres is beaten unconscious and his body is dumped along the river.

Isa meets up with Jack Normanton at the park and gives him Don Chailey's photographs. He says that the photographs will make the front page on newspapers around the world.

Beto has arranged for himself and Isa to perform at the San Jose orphanage. Isa is reluctant to leave Santiago when Andres is missing. Beto fears that Andres is coming between them, but Isa reassures him that she can love both of them.

Andres manages to move himself away from the other dead bodies along the river. He is saved by a farmer and his daughter.

A week after the assassination of Miguel Alberti, Santiago is under military occupation and all vehicles coming in and out of the city are inspected. Andres makes it safely to the market in the back of Francisco's van. He thinks he is dying, but is inspired when he learns that his friends are performing at the market. Rosa helps him hide in the back of the twin's van. Isa and Beto avoid arrest twice and are reunited with Andres when they stop for lunch at the quarry.

A short time later, the stadium of Santiago is cleaned up and the Two Hemispheres Trophy is played between Chile and England. There are no traces of the suffering and death which took place here. General Zuckerman watches the game from the State Box. Earlier in the day he had reprimanded the Archbishop of Santiago for suggesting that Security was involved in the death of Father Mariano. The Director of State Information Services disturbs General Zuckerman to show him the front page of the *Baltimore Express & Times* which carries a story by Jack Normanton and a huge picture of Miguel Alberti at the moment of his assassination. All over the stadium of Santiago leaflets are also being distributed featuring Don Chailey's photographs and testimony of the assassination of the Silver Lion. These same leaflets are being distributed all over Chile. Andres loves Isa and watches her circulate the leaflets in the stands. He thinks of his father. There are tears in his eyes but they are of hope as well as despair.

Who? What? Why? When? Where? How?

1 Isa, Beto and Andres.
2 Isa read out the details of Don Chailey's press card.
3 Tonio, Francisco's son and Rosa's brother, killed by the CNI.
4 They think that he was running a message to Diego Rosales from his comrade Hernando.
5 The Archbishop of Santiago.
6 They create a distraction and, through shear numbers, create a human barrier between the Black Berets and the twins' van.
7 To cover the elections.
8 The opening match of the Two Hemispheres Trophy.
9 At the quarry where they first picked up Andres and ate with him.
10 The reporter says that Chailey has not been seen since Monday night.

Who says that, and to whom?

1 The Director of the State Information Services to General Zuckerman, showing him the morning edition of the *Baltimore Express & Times*. The Epilogue.

2   The Snake to the Hog, taking responsibility for Father Mariano's death. Chapter 7.
3   Francisco yells at Andres to stop singing as they approach a road block. Chapter 8.
4   Francisco to Rosa about helping Andres. Chapter 7.
5   General Zuckerman to the Archbishop of Santiago. The Epilogue.
6   Rosa to Andres. Chapter 8.
7   Jack Normanton to Isa, exclaiming how interested the rest of the world will be in Don Chailey's photographs. Chapter 7.
8   Andres lets Beto know that he is in the van. Chapter 8.
9   The puppet General Zuckero to the crowd. Chapter 8.
10 Colonel Rugeros to Jack Normanton and another reporter. Chapter 7.

Open quotes
1   'Tonio had no one to help him… he would want us to help this boy.' Rosa to her father about helping Andres. Chapter 7.
2   'I'm not going to answer a stranger's questions unless I'm given the secret password.' 'I'm talking in whispers… will that do?' Jack Normanton and Isa exchange the password when they meet. Chapter 7.
3   'Any passengers in the back?' 'Not at the last count, Officer.' Beto replying to the Black Beret when he asks if anyone is in the back of the van – Beto is ignorant that Andres is hidden there. Chapter 8.
4   'You, Sis have gone crazy!… But am I proud of you!' Beto to Isa about her bravery during the puppet show at the San Miguel market. Chapter 8.
5   'Order in Chile has been restored: the right order; and all's right with the world.' Watson, the author, is commenting ironically on General Zuckerman's relaxed air at the start of the football match. The Epilogue.
6   'They could have shot me for cheek.' 'True, Beto. But I loved you for it!' Beto and Isa reflect on their near escape from being arrested. Chapter 8.
7   'You think Andres has come between us – that I'm more concerned about him than I am about you?' Isa to Beto during their argument over Andres. Chapter 7.
8   'Is it sleep – or something worse?' Andres wonders to himself if he is dying. Chapter 8.
9   'For old time's sake… we'll have our lunch where we first broke bread with Towny.' Beto to Isa about stopping for lunch by the quarry. Chapter 8.
10 'Did Mariano make his confession?' 'To his Maker, Sir… But not to us.' The Snake and the messenger on whether Father Mariano made a confession before he died. Chapter 7.

Notes

Notes

Notes

Notes

Notes